An Everlasting Gift

An Everlasting Gift

*Celebrating the Eucharist
in Today's Church*

**Edward Dowler and
Brendan Clover**

TUFTON
BOOKS

Text © Edward Dowler and Brendan Clover 2004

First published in 2004 for Tufton Books,
the publishing imprint of the Church Union,
by the Canterbury Press, Norwich
(a publishing imprint of Hymns Ancient & Modern Limited,
a registered charity)
St Mary's Works, St Mary's Plain,
Norwich, Norfolk, NR3 3BH

www.scm-canterburypress.co.uk

British Library Cataloguing in Publication data

A catalogue record for this book is available
from the British Library

ISBN 1-85191-052-1

Typeset by Regent Typesetting
Printed and bound by
Biddles Ltd, www.biddles.co.uk

Contents

Contents

Acknowledgements

The authors were enormously helped by friends and colleagues who read this book at various different stages, commented upon it and made suggestions for how it might be improved. Among others, they would like to thank Jane Ball, Sister Margaret ASSP, Fr Timothy Pike CR, Jill Pinnock, Jeremy Sheehy, Carrie Thompson, John Thompson-Vear and Alan Wakeley. They would also like to thank the communities of St Stephen's House, Oxford, and Bristol Cathedral for their ongoing support through the time of writing.

Foreword by the
Archbishop of York

As Archbishop of York I have the enormous privilege of attending magnificent and moving services in churches and cathedrals in the province and more widely. While such celebrations are memorable, I always look forward to the opportunity of presiding at a parish Eucharist and taking time to meet with the clergy and people who, day by day and week by week, keep the rumour of God alive through their prayerfulness, their corporate worship and their maintenance of the many parish churches up and down the country.

In this book, Edward Dowler and Brendan Clover have produced a work designed for parish churches that will allow clergy and people to review their worship theologically and liturgically, so that God may receive the best that a community can offer, and congregations may be drawn closer to God and to each other through the eucharistic celebration.

The book is comprehensive in its scope – from suggestions about altar wine to historical background on liturgical texts and garments. This breadth and the clarity of presentation will enable the book to be used and reused as a tool for liturgical review and renewal. It will also prove to be an extremely valuable resource for newly ordained clergy and particularly those preparing for ordination as priests.

The two key words in the book are ones that I would echo from my own experience of seeking to plan and order liturgy, namely, simplicity and dignity. I believe if these two elements are reflected in the celebration of the Holy Eucharist then something of the mysterious transcendence of the God, who in Christ meets us in the blessed sacrament of the altar, will be conveyed and communicated.

+David Ebor
Archbishop of York

Introduction

May he make us an everlasting gift to you
and enable us to share in the inheritance of your saints.

Eucharistic Prayer III, Roman Rite

This book is not intended to be a scholarly volume on liturgy or, indeed, sacramental theology. It is a simple guide to the celebration of the Eucharist in the modern catholic tradition of the Church of England.* We hope that it will be useful for individual and group study and will stimulate reflection and discussion in parishes and other worshipping communities. We hope that it will help to encourage eucharistic worship that combines dignity and accessibility and that this will thereby contribute to the Church's mission.

Why the Need for Such a Book?

The official liturgy of the Church of England, the *Book of Common Prayer*, gives quite explicit instructions about things such as the ordering of churches and about liturgical actions and gestures. However, in the newer Anglican liturgies, such as the *Alternative Service Book* (*ASB*, now superseded) and the set of books that now make up *Common Worship*, no such instructions exist. The result of this is a great diversity of liturgical practice, some of which enriches the life of the Church and some of which causes puzzlement and difficulty. Our aim here is to provide a basic set of norms, not as

* Particular reference is made to Order One of *Common Worship, Services and Prayers for the Church of England*.

unbreakable rules, since we are in no position to make any such rules, but rather as guidelines for good practice. Such guidelines we hope will foster rather than suppress the creativity that is always a part of good liturgy.

The book is designed in such a way as to make its recommendations reasonably easy to implement in any parish setting. We will not be suggesting massive reordering schemes or buying new and expensive items (in fact, if anything, we will tend to suggest that certain objects be discarded rather than acquired). Throughout, we try to take account not just of what is ideal but of what is, in practical terms, possible in communities that have limited resources.

It is hoped that the book might provide the basis for reflection and discussion groups in parishes and other communities wishing to review their eucharistic worship. In order to facilitate this, questions are provided at the end of each chapter. In view of the sensitivities that liturgical topics often arouse, these exercises will need to be carefully handled and set within their proper framework.

What are the Guiding Principles?

Simplicity

The 'Liturgical Movement' that grew up in the twentieth century, given impetus by the Second Vatican Council but spanning all the main Christian denominations, drew attention to the importance of simplicity in liturgical celebrations. Although this development towards greater simplicity has been questioned by some Church historians and liturgical scholars, this book presupposes that the liturgy will be celebrated in a relatively simple and straightforward manner. Thus we recommend, as will be explained below, a tidy and uncluttered liturgical space; simplicity and economy of movement and gesture and the minimum possible fussiness of any kind. We believe that liturgy celebrated in a simple, prayerful way is most likely to maintain the focus of the congregation upon God.

Dignity

Combined with simplicity, we also believe in the importance of worship and, in particular, the Eucharist having a certain dignity. Such a view may be contested by those who believe that many people are put off Christian worship by its perceived stiffness and formality. While we understand the strength of this opinion, we write in the conviction that in the Eucharist something very important indeed is happening and that the awe and wonder of this event are best nurtured by a certain dignity in the service. Such a dignity is very different to stiff and unbending formality, something that is indeed alienating and off-putting. However, we also believe that people can be alienated by a lack of reverence and excessive 'mateyness' in church services. In this pamphlet, we will suggest that the Eucharist be celebrated in a warm and accessible way which, ideally, will reflect and re-enforce relationships in the Christian community, but that such warmth and accessibility should be combined with dignity and due reverence to the wonderful things that God is doing in the midst of those who celebrate this sacrament.

Focus of the Book

From the outset, this book has been intended to have quite a limited scope and we are very well aware of what might seem like some major omissions in the material we present.

The participation of children in the Eucharist is only occasionally discussed. The reason for this is not that it is unimportant – quite the contrary – but rather that it is simply too big a subject for this size of book. We hope, however, that the simple and uncluttered approach that we argue for will help commend the Eucharist to Christians of all ages.

The celebration of the seasons is only partially touched on, as this, again, is a big subject which requires another book to do it justice. Our primary focus here is on the 'normal': on 'Ordinary time' and the Sunday by Sunday worship in Christian communities.

We have also chosen not to focus explicitly on what is sometimes called the *emerging Church*. We tend to assume that, for example, a church building exists, whereas in reality many churches in the future (as in the early Church) will meet in houses and halls and not in specially designated buildings. All we can say to this is that we hope that many of our suggestions will be applicable in a number of settings.

A final thing that should be said is that we do not offer this book out of any conceited sense that we have got liturgy right and everyone else has got it wrong. Indeed, we are both all too keenly aware of the liturgical shortcomings of the communities in which we have worked and worshipped, some at least of which have been directly due to ourselves. What we hope we can offer is reflection on eucharistic practice experienced in a variety of settings and our prayerful attempts to discern how the people of God are called to offer it in today's Church.

The 'everlasting gift' of which the title of this book speaks is not in fact the Eucharist. The Eucharist is, like all the sacraments, a gift that will no longer be needed when Christ returns in glory. And yet, the Eucharist points us forward to that which is everlasting: to the Kingdom of God, inaugurated by Christ; that Kingdom which is both present and still to come. As we wait for the Kingdom that the Eucharist foreshadows, through that same Eucharist Christ is making his people an everlasting gift to the Father.

Edward Dowler

Brendan Clover

Part 1

People

I

The Congregation

Role in the Service

Holy Communion is celebrated by the whole people of God gathered for worship. The ministry of the members of the congregation is expressed through their active participation together in the words and actions of the service.

Common Worship, Services and Prayers for the Church of England, p. 158

As a Second Vatican Council statement says, the Eucharist is a celebration of the whole Church in which each baptized person should participate fully, consciously and actively. Although people have been saying this for quite a long time, it is very rare that you go to a church (of any tradition) and feel that it actually happens. Far more often, people make comments such as 'Father X was taking the service', implying that the clergy and choir *produced* a liturgical product that everyone else *consumed*. Often it is assumed that the word 'congregation' means the people sitting in the pews whereas, in fact, it describes the entire 'assembly': all who are present and celebrating the Eucharist together.

In many ways, the intention of this book is to encourage greater participation by the whole people of God in the celebration of the Eucharist. This is done by attention to, for example, the space in which the congregation meets for worship, the way that readings are read and sermons constructed, the symbols that are used to draw people into the action of the

service, the books that people are given to help them participate.

However, there is one danger that a participatory approach
to worship can bring, which is that it can leave people with
very little space. Those who are unfamiliar or uncommitted
may not wish to be drawn immediately into something that
they are still uncertain about, but rather to have some time to
'taste and see that the Lord is good' (Ps. 34.8). Thus, good
liturgy, as well as creating opportunities for full participation,
will always give people space and freedom.

One of the authors of this book had a fellow curate who
was once approached by a young woman who said that she
would like to go to church but wasn't sure what to do. The
curate's response was, 'Do whatever you like!' In one sense, of
course, in a corporate act of worship it is important that
people should *not* all be doing different things but, in another,
the point is well made and in some ways the very purpose of
liturgical structures is to allow people freedom within them.

Response

As well as bodily participation in movement and posture,
vocal participation is important as well. In many churches, the
response to, for example, the greeting 'The Lord be with you'
is very weak and feeble. Just as musical preparation is sometimes needed for a congregation, speaking preparation may
also be useful from time to time. People need encouragement
to answer strongly and loudly.

Teaching Point

The 'Great Amen'

The word *Amen* is derived from a Hebrew word meaning
something like 'truly'. In the Gospels, especially in John,

Jesus is often presented as using the Greek version of the word in his characteristic teaching formula, 'Truly, I say to you ...' *Amen* is, of course, familiar as the congregational response to many prayers, hymns and affirmations of faith (Deut. 27.15 and 1 Cor. 14.16).

Although the word 'Amen' will be used a number of times in any celebration of the Eucharist, the 'Great Amen' at the end of the Eucharistic Prayer has a special significance. For, from the earliest days of the Church, this is the time when members of the congregation together give joint assent to all that has happened. It is the climax of the Eucharistic Prayer. It is for this reason that the Great Amen in the Eucharist should be a joyful acclamation of praise. Unfortunately, it is often just a low murmur and needs encouragement and perhaps even the use of a musical setting to draw out its significance.

Another reason for lack of response is that people can be unclear about what they are meant to be saying at different times. A later chapter on Books aims to give guidance on making this as clear as possible.

Movement

Since human beings are embodied, physical creatures, participation is enhanced if the congregation does not remain entirely static through the service. Physical participation is always important in the Eucharist, hence the importance of practices such as making the sign of the cross, joining in with processions, and so on.

In almost all churches, members of the congregation will stand, sit and perhaps kneel at different points in the Eucharist, but at which points should these things happen?

The key thing is that posture should fit in an obvious way

with the liturgical action (for example, sitting attentively for the sermon, standing to honour the gospel, etc.). There should perhaps be a certain theological bias in favour of standing, as this is what we are able to do in the light of the resurrection (in the words of the Eucharistic Prayer, 'We thank you for counting us worthy to stand in your presence and serve you'). However, the attitudes of humility and reverence that are implied by kneeling are also, of course, vital. It is also very important that people are not going up and down like jack-in-the-boxes.

A basic suggestion which attempts to match the considerations listed above might be:

- Stand for the gathering, the penitential rite and the collect.
- Sit for the readings and psalm.
- Stand for the alleluia and gospel.
- Sit for the sermon.
- Stand for the creed, the intercessions and the peace.
- Stand for the Eucharistic Prayer, the Lord's Prayer and the Agnus Dei.
- Sit or kneel before or after receiving communion.
- Stand for the prayer after communion, blessing and dismissal.

In some settings, congregations will not only adjust their posture but actually move around the church at some point. This might be to gather around the altar for the Eucharistic Prayer or perhaps to move to different places for different parts of the service (the font, for example, to gather and confess sins, the lectern for the Liturgy of the Word, the altar for the Liturgy of the Sacrament). This will enhance the sense that the people of God are on a pilgrimage and not, as it often seems, simply static. However, there are undoubtedly problems, in sizeable congregations, with trying to move large numbers of people around.

Two further points are:

• It is also important always to remember in relation to questions of posture and movement (and, indeed, the construction of liturgical space) that some members of the congregation will be more mobile than others.
• In congregations where literacy is poor, or where English is not everyone's first language, movement and gesture can be a powerful tool for participation, unity and inclusion: the importance of these things should not be underestimated or regarded as one of the 'inessentials'.

Prayer

Finally and crucially, participation in the Eucharist means that people need to be able to pray in it. Many find this extremely difficult and quite a few have given up even trying. It is very difficult to be prescriptive about this but church communities need to ask themselves quite regularly what it is about the building, the interaction of people, the music, the words, that helps to create a prayerful atmosphere and what are the things that destroy such an atmosphere.

Similarly, it is the responsibility of those leading worship to find ways to establish the prayerful atmosphere that will help the whole congregation make the transition into worship. This can be helped by the clergy or servers having a period of silent prayer before the Eucharist begins or perhaps by some music being played or sung. Important though this is, it is unlikely to be achieved by the clergy hectoring people not to talk to one another before the service begins. Subtle methods are likely to achieve more.

A prayerful atmosphere, of course, should not simply be equated with absolute quietness or stillness (a particularly important point when children are in evidence). The Eucharist offers a chance to express the full gamut of praying 'moods', from quiet and reflective to loud and praising. A Sunday

Parish Eucharist can create a number of different moods and atmospheres.

Care Before and After

It is outside the scope of this book to give very detailed comments on this subject except to point out that the celebration of the Eucharist does not happen in a vacuum. Thus, it is clearly important that people of all sorts find a generous welcome when they come to the Eucharist and, if necessary, have the service explained to them. It is also important to establish good after-service care. This will normally include high-quality refreshments, nicely served (in other words, not powdered coffee and milk served in a plastic cup accompanied by soft digestive biscuits). Where possible, members of the congregation should be especially designated and trained to make people feel welcomed and included.

Questions for Reflection and Discussion

- How can people participate more fully in the Parish Eucharist in your church?
- How easy is it for newcomers or visitors to 'taste and see'?
- What sort of movement happens in the service and does this need to be reviewed?
- How easy is it to pray at the Sunday Eucharist in your church?
- How satisfactory are the arrangements for welcome and after-service care?

2

The President

Teaching Point

The president

The president at the Eucharist is the bishop or, if (as often) he cannot be present, one of the priests to whom the bishop has delegated his presiding role.

There are various different words for the president at the Eucharist, none of which is without problems. Of these, the word 'president', most commonly used in Anglican liturgies, has connotations of political leadership. The word 'celebrant', often used in the Roman Catholic Church, detracts from the fact that the whole 'assembly' are celebrants at the Eucharist and not just the presiding priest or bishop. The word 'presider' is (arguably) not an English word at all! The word 'priest' describes a particular ministry but not a role in the Eucharist.

Despite difficulties of nomenclature, the task of the president, as envisaged by modern liturgical texts, is a very important one. The president is a little like the conductor of an orchestra or the person chairing a meeting. It is the president's job to co-ordinate the actions of the congregation so that the worship can truly be a communal offering to God. It is no more the president's job to do everything in the service than it is the conductor's to play every instrument in the concert.

All members of the congregation should be encouraged to play a full part in the Eucharist but the role of presiding *throughout the service* belongs to the president and to the president alone. By contrast with a possible interpretation of the provisions of the *Alternative Service Book* (cf. p. 115, n. 2), the *Common Worship* rubric emphasizes that,

> The unity of the liturgy is served by the ministry of the president, who *in presiding over the whole service* holds word and sacrament together and draws the congregation into a worshipping community (our italics).

This means that it is not appropriate for a deacon, a lay person or indeed another priest to preside over the Liturgy of the Word and the president over the Liturgy of the Sacrament, since word and sacrament form a vital unity.

If a priest is unable to preside over the Eucharist in its entirety, another service is always more appropriate. *Common Worship* provision for a Service of the Word with extended communion is presumably intended to meet this need.

The president's role in the Eucharist will best be fulfilled when three vital aspects of it are considered: manner, words and actions.

Manner

Setting the right tone

Within a few seconds of the beginning of the Eucharist, the tone is set by the person presiding. This will be done by the way they move, their manner of speech and their mode of interaction with the rest of the congregation. If the president is formal and pompous, it is likely to give the message that the Eucharist is part of a 'churchy' world, unrelated to people's everyday lives and experiences. If, on the other hand, the president is casual and careless, it will give the message that the Eucharist really doesn't matter either to the president or to anyone else. It is necessary then for the president to set a tone that is easy and natural but also reverent and prayerful. This should communicate that the Eucharist takes place among those whom Jesus calls friends (John 15.15) but also that it concerns the holy, the mysterious, the transcendent.

Establishing the right relationships

The president at the Eucharist functions within the worshipping community so relationships with other members of the congregation are vital. In particular, the president needs to interact well with the other 'key players' in the celebration – servers, readers, intercessor, musicians – so that there is a sense that all are working in harmony. Good eucharistic presidency involves allowing other people in the assembly to fulfil the roles that are rightly theirs. It also involves working hard to channel people's attention towards God and not obtruding one's own personality in distracting ways. However, having said all this, the president does need to preside: to 'hold' the celebration so that a space is created for each person to play their own part.

Words

The president has different types of words to say at different points in the Eucharist. These require a somewhat different register. They include:

Welcome

Order One states that 'words of welcome or introduction may be said' after the celebrant has greeted the people. It is emphasized that these words come *after* the initial greeting (that is, 'The Lord be with you', or equivalent) and *not* before it, because it is surely right that, in the context of worship, a greeting in the name of God should precede the president's own greeting.

However, the president's own words of greeting and introduction to the Eucharist are nonetheless important. The space provided here to say some opening words of welcome and introduction are a very good opportunity for the president, in a couple of sentences (though probably no more), to set the right tone and establish from the outset a good liturgical relationship with the rest of the congregation, introducing the theme of the readings and perhaps also saying something about the purpose of the Eucharist. This opportunity should not be wasted.

Prayers

When it comes to the words of prayers, such as the collect and the Eucharistic Prayer, people are likely to be strongly put off by any sort of 'parsonical voice'. Also, the days in which it was thought that these prayers (or parts of them) should be said in an expressionless monotone are now over. Congregations will respond well to prayers being spoken in a way that is natural and not artificially impregnated with meaning, but one that is also prayerful and sounds sincere.

Part of the president's role of leading the whole congregation in prayer includes establishing periods of prayerful silence. Times at which this is especially important are:

- between the words 'Let us pray' and the collect
- after the sermon
- after communion.

Notices

Common Worship does not suggest any particular stage in the service for notices to be given. In many churches, it is done right at the start of the Eucharist. This is surely not an appropriate time. The congregation have gathered in order to

worship God, not to hear notices, and worship should therefore be the obvious primary thing. By contrast, if notices are
given first, the message conveyed is that these are primary. A
much better time for notices is near the end of the Eucharist,
between the prayer after communion and the blessing.

Although notices are a functional part of the service, they
are nonetheless a sort of evangelistic opportunity because the
president has an opportunity to talk to the congregation in a
more relaxed and informal way than at other times. This may
well be important for those not used to the relative formality
of liturgical worship. However, the notices take place within
the Eucharist and so it is appropriate that they should not be
over-long and that they should not be a point at which the dignity of the Eucharist is suddenly dropped. In some parishes,
members of the congregation are invited to give notices and
this can help reinforce a sense of the corporate nature of the
church.

Announcements

Announcements of, for example, hymn numbers, pages in the
service book, the posture people should take ('we now sit ...')
and so on puncture the prayerfulness and disrupt the flow
of the liturgy and so these need to be kept to an *absolute
minimum*.

Actions

From the time that Jesus took, blessed, broke and distributed
the bread and wine at the Last Supper, actions and not just
words have been vital to the way the Eucharist is celebrated.
Later on, the actions that are appropriate at different times
will be described in more detail. However, in this section it is
worth drawing attention to some basic principles. Actions at
the Eucharist broadly fall into two types, movements (using
the whole body) and gestures (using just the hands).

Movements

Fussy, exaggerated or over-precise movements by eucharistic presidents or others are all great turn-offs to other members of the congregation. Among such movements are the 'catholic corners' that are still seen in some churches (that is, turning at ninety-degree angles when in or approaching the sanctuary), huge swings of a thurible either by servers or clergy and processions moving at a pace of funereal slowness. All this looks affected and often ridiculous. Movement in church should be natural but dignified and unhurried. This will draw attention not to the liturgical 'leaders' but to God and will help create the right atmosphere. In addition, the creation of the right type of liturgical space (see chapter 11) will greatly aid natural and dignified movement.

Further distraction is caused when the president is continually moving around and some *economy of movement* is important in this respect. If the president's chair is situated in a suitable position (see chapter 11), then this is surely the right place from which to preside *at all times*, either sitting down or standing up – except when the president is sharing the peace, standing behind the altar or distributing communion. There is no need for the president to be, for example, turning round to say the creed, kneeling in front of the altar for the prayer after communion or marching to the front of the altar to introduce the peace.

Gestures

Gestures that are simple and ample but not exaggerated will draw the congregation into the action of the Eucharist. If the sign of the cross is going to be made, for example, it should be across the whole body. If the hands are going to be stretched out, they should be stretched out reasonably wide. Like movements, gestures can seem natural and dignified or they can seem affected and fussy. In some churches, it is still possible to experience very fussy manual actions over the bread and wine which, again, are distracting and offputting. The final section of this book will make more specific suggestions for these to be done in a simple but effective way.

Questions for Reflection and Discussion

- What qualities do you think are important in a president of the Eucharist?
- How can the rest of the congregation help the president to preside more effectively?
- Why are movement and gesture important in the Eucharist? How do they happen in your church?

Teaching Point

The deacon

Traditionally, the role of deacons in the Eucharist has been an extremely important one. In the early Church, Ignatius of Antioch (c. 35 – c.107) talks of 'deacons of the mysteries of God', presumably a reference to their central role in the liturgy. Some early church bishops, such as the famous Cyprian of Carthage in North Africa (d. 258) would not celebrate the Eucharist unless a deacon was present to fulfil the diaconal functions. The role of deacons in the Eucharist has varied in all traditions but it includes proclamation of the gospel, preparing the bread and wine and taking the consecrated elements to those who are sick. In addition, the deacon has an 'enabling' role: inviting the congregation, for example, to share the sign of peace or sending people out to 'Go in peace to love and serve the Lord'.

In the view of the authors of this book, the Church needs a renewed 'permanent' diaconate (that is, not one that is simply a stepping stone to priestly ordination). It would be of great benefit to the Church if there were a deacon in every parish or group of parishes, exercising what the authors of a recent report on the subject describe as a non-presidential ministry of 'word, sacrament and pastoral care'. Because many parishes do not have deacons, the diaconal role is often carried out by a lay person acting as a 'liturgical deacon'. Although this is not ideal, it is perhaps preferable to the president being over-dominant. However, the deacon should not take on a quasi-presidential role in the Eucharist (such as leading the Liturgy of the Word) since this is an unhelpful confusion of roles.

Further reading on the deacon's role is suggested in the bibliography.

3

Servers and Eucharistic Ministers

In most churches where the Eucharist is the central Sunday service, there is likely to be some sort of serving team. This can vary in size from a solitary individual who always does it to a large group, organized on a rota basis.

Describing the Servers' Role in the Eucharist

Necessity

Perhaps the first question to ask about servers is whether they are really necessary. Some would argue that tasks that have traditionally been given to servers, such as bringing gifts and incense to the altar, carrying the cross in procession and assisting with the distribution of communion, should not be the preserve of an élite, semi-clerical team but rightly belong to the whole people of God who should be enlisted as and when necessary. Churches which meet in non-ecclesial settings (such as school halls and community centres) and churches where there are few people who wish to be servers, or where the serving team has become tired and static, might well try this approach.

However, although dispensing with servers altogether might be thought to have both attractions and theological justification, it may not be entirely practical. In almost all churches, in order to ensure smooth running and confident participation in the liturgy, it is likely that there will be a team of people dedicated to assisting the rest of the congregation to worship by attending to the 'nuts and bolts' of liturgical arrangements. Because of this role, in many churches, servers are a crucial part of the liturgical ministry who do a vital job of 'enabling' on behalf of the entire congregation.

Best and worst

One of the authors of this book, when he was a student, went to the Parish Eucharist at a church in a very deprived housing estate in an African/Afro-Caribbean part of west London. Before going there, he had always been used to serving teams being made up of slightly precious looking men who seemed to be walking on tramlines. However, in this church, although the serving team was composed of somewhat ramshackle teenagers, the servers gave the impression that they were all working *together*, with one another, with the priest and with the rest of the congregation. Moreover, they had an obvious happiness and pride in what they were doing and did not have the gloomy expressions that are commonly seen on servers' faces. Here was not the perfect liturgical 'choreography' on which some churches pride themselves and yet all the servers clearly knew what they were supposed to be doing in the service of God at each stage of the Eucharist and they went about these tasks with dignity and reverence.

By contrast, in another parish where one of the authors has worked, there was a serving team that was meticulously well-rehearsed, choreographed and organized on a rota basis. The curate, however, noticed that one server seemed at various parts of the service always to be writing in a book. Slightly surprised and wondering whether, perhaps, the man was sketching one of the windows, the curate asked him what he did in these parts of the Eucharist. The server, who was a teacher, said that he used the spare time in the service to mark his pupils' essays.

Tasks

Servers vary enormously from place to place and it would be impossible to design a 'one-size-fits-all' programme, but the normal things that servers are enlisted to do include:

- Preparing the church for worship.
- Leading in with cross, candles, incense, etc. at the entrance procession.
- Assisting the president with the book at the chair.
- Helping to honour the gospel reading with candles, incense, etc.
- Assisting with the setting up of the altar at the offertory.
- Assisting with communion, e.g. by administering a chalice.
- Assisting with the ablutions after communion and helping to clear the altar.
- Leading out at the end of the service.
- Tidying up the church after the service.

In all churches, it is helpful to reflect on precisely how and why these things are done, to ensure that they happen with simplicity and dignity.

Questions about the Servers' Role in the Eucharist

These stories and others like them prompt several questions that are always useful to consider.

What is the serving team's relationship to the congregation?

In most churches, servers have an important role in facilitating and enabling the worship of the entire congregation. The role of servers, however, is *never* to become themselves the focus of attention. Behaviours that deflect attention from the liturgy and towards particular individuals (and, among these, might be included fussily lifting up the president's chasuble at various points in the service, exaggeratedly precise movements, excessive slowness or obvious bossiness) have no place in the Eucharist. Fundamentally, the entire congregation including the servers and indeed the president are there for worship and therefore need to keep this as a sense of common purpose. Servers are there to help the entire people of God participate in the liturgy.

What is the serving team's relationship to the president?

The servers and the president need to relate to one another in a natural and friendly way. This is a reciprocal relationship. On the one hand, the president should not, as is sometimes seen, appear to treat servers in a peremptory or curt manner. The president should give the impression that servers are valued members of the community whose contributions are important, even when they get things wrong. On the other hand, servers need to foster a mentality in which they don't simply do their jobs but are aware of the liturgy as a whole and the president's role within it, and are able to step in if something needs to be done to ensure the smooth running of the service.

In practical terms, teamwork between presidents and servers can be fostered by small touches such as a server holding the president's book at the chair, when this is needed, and servers and president being trained to be sensitive to one another so that it can easily be indicated that something needs to be done without a great performance that disrupts the liturgy.

How are servers selected and trained?

Many different people can be servers and it is surprising what relationships can be forged across age groups by people united in this task. Some commentators discourage the use of children who have recently been confirmed but, if people in this category are keen to do the job, then why not? Far better for servers to be keen members of the church who occasionally make mistakes than more disciplined people who would rather be marking essays. Importantly, servers represent the laity and if they reflect the diversity of the congregation in terms of age, gender, ethnicity, etc., this will give strong messages about the aims and priorities of a particular church community.

As with all liturgical ministers, servers need proper training to be enabled to fulfil their role. There is no substitute for proper training sessions, perhaps linked with some social event. Such events will also help to foster the sense of teamwork among them. A training session is the time for servers to be corrected and guided. During the liturgy itself, such correction and guidance will always be a distraction.

What do they wear?

The dignity of eucharistic worship is enhanced if servers wear distinctive clothing. Servers are highly visible in the liturgy and their clothing (like that of the president) should not detract from the focus upon God. There are practical reasons too for having some kind of 'uniform', since this will avoid having to explain why, for example, shorts, white plimsolls, high heels and so on are inappropriate (as indeed they are).

Perhaps the best garment for servers is a simple white or cream alb which, theologically, is the garment of the baptized and, practically speaking, is elegant and easy to keep clean.

Where do they sit?

The importance of a prominent position for the president's chair, in which the president really can preside, is emphasized in chapter 11. This cannot happen if the president and servers are all sitting together in a row nor is there any reason why servers, whose role in the liturgy is basically a functional one (carrying, enabling, facilitating), should occupy centre stage in a way that would detract attention from the 'action' of the liturgy at the lectern or the altar. However, the president and servers need to be fairly near to each other at all times so that they can work as a team and establish eye contact if necessary. Generally, it will be best for servers to sit on some designated seating to one side of the altar.

Questions for Reflection and Discussion

- What are the different ways of serving that you have experienced and how have they helped or hindered worship?
- How do the servers work in your church? Which of the issues discussed in this chapter might need attention?

Part 2

Words

4

Books

The arrival of *Common Worship* has undoubtedly led the Church of England into a new liturgical era. The days when one service book would suffice for all services are, for better or for worse, over. Now, it is up to individual parishes, using the great variety of texts on offer, to work out which options will be used and how. The benefits of this development are obvious: greater flexibility in liturgical texts, richer variety and so on. There are, however, drawbacks as well. One of these is that the availability of so many options can detract from a feeling that the liturgy is, in some sense, *given* and *shared*. Another disadvantage is that many people (particularly but not exclusively clergy and readers) who may not have a natural aptitude for liturgy are forced to become liturgists because of the enormous responsibilities that they now have for deciding which texts are used and when.

It is not within the scope of this book to give detailed guidance about which of the many options that *Common Worship* offers should be used for different parts of the Eucharist (although some comments on this are offered in part 5 on movement). In general, it is sensible to make use of the available material but not to overdo it. Stability and rhythm are spiritually important as well as variety and interest.

This chapter will aim to provide some guidance about the ways that the different liturgical materials can be presented so that they can be used by congregations without too much difficulty and confusion. It will concentrate on the books that are generally thought necessary for celebrating the Eucharist:

the congregational book or pamphlet, the book(s) that the president uses, the lectionary and the book of the Gospels.

Congregational Books

Type of book

Almost all churches have some sort of basic service book that enables people to follow the Eucharist. It is strongly recommended that churches should *not* give people the entire volume *Common Worship: Services and Prayers for the Church of England*. Not only is this too bulky and unwieldy for everyday use but also, despite its very careful and professional layout, it is simply too complex to expect anyone without liturgical training to find their way through it during a service. Obviously, it is good for this book to be available if people would like to look at it but, for everyday use, it will be better to have service books that come either in booklet or pamphlet form.

* Booklets with words for the Eucharist are available in the *Common Worship* series. These have the advantage of not creating extra work since they can easily be bought and they include all the available options. Their *disadvantage*, however, is that the number of different options and variations is likely to make them difficult to follow. In practice, many churches opt for locally produced books which can be adapted to reflect the usage of a particular church and perhaps also contain illustrations and devotional material that will be helpful to worshippers. In some churches, a booklet will be produced for every Sunday Eucharist, complete with hymns, readings, prayers, etc. This, of course, makes the service very easy to follow but it is time-consuming to produce and wasteful of money and paper.

* Pamphlets containing the words of the Eucharist are also available from various sources or they can be printed

locally. It is quite possible for all the words that the congregation needs to fit comfortably into a pamphlet of A4 size, folded into two or three. Different pamphlets can then be produced for different seasons and occasions without adding complexity. Pamphlets need to be made of good quality card, perhaps of different colours to reflect the different seasons.

Whichever type of service book is thought appropriate, some important considerations always apply:

Professionalism

In the era of word processing and desktop publishing, it is no longer acceptable for service booklets or pamphlets to be dog-eared, badly printed or to contain typographical errors. It is likewise not acceptable for mistakes in liturgical material to be corrected by crossing out and correcting by hand or by sticking small pieces of paper over words or sentences. People are used, in all areas of life, to smartly produced literature that looks professional and it will convey a very poor impression if they do not receive such literature when they come to church. Whether the words for the Eucharist are to be printed in booklet or pamphlet form, it needs to be a professional or semi-professional job. With advances in computer technology, doing such a job is now within the competence of many people and need not be expensive. With the *Common Worship* material, texts can easily be downloaded from the internet, avoiding the need for extra typing.

Professional compilation of these materials will always take into account:

- Legibility (considering the font and the point size).
- Layout (considering the speech rhythms and the way things are said).
- The needs of those who, for whatever reason, find reading English difficult (large print, Braille, bilingual texts etc.).

- The needs of children (which means considering such things as special cards or booklets).

Simplicity

People who produce service booklets and pamphlets need, at all times, to try and make the Eucharist as simple as possible to follow. To those who are not familiar with the liturgy (and even to some who are), it is thoroughly confusing to have to flick this way and that through a complicated book in order to find the right place. It is also confusing for many to have to wade through seasonal variations (such as 'In Lent only we say ...' or 'In Eastertide, the following may be added ...'). If different texts are being used, it will therefore almost always be best to produce different materials. This will also reduce the need for superfluous announcements of page or paragraph numbers (for example, 'We will now turn to the second prayer on page 169 for the confession'), which always detract from the prayerfulness of the service.

Explanation

Service booklets and pamphlets do *not* need to contain a large amount of explanation of movement and action. It is unnecessary to say, for example, that 'the president makes the sign of the cross'. So far as movements are concerned, it is better just to do them and let them speak for themselves. It is also unnecessary for the Eucharistic Prayer to be printed out in full since the effect of this will be to keep eyes glued to the page.

Generally speaking, the more that people can be encouraged to take their eyes away from the book and experience the Eucharist as the corporate and visual act of worship that it is, the better. The congregational booklet or pamphlet really only needs to contain the words that the congregation says or sings at various points in the Eucharist. If explanation is needed (as it often is) then this can be written out separately or conveyed in a study group or 'teaching' Eucharist.

Structure

One of the important characteristics of modern eucharistic rites is their insistence on the clear structure of the service. The fact that such a structure exists is not always obvious to worshippers, who often experience the service as 'just one damn thing after another'. The appropriate use of headings, booklets and pamphlets can emphasize the fact that the Eucharist has a clear structure and sense of momentum and familiarize people with key terms such as gathering, Liturgy of the Word, Liturgy of the Sacrament and dismissal.

Number

Whatever type of service book is used, churches need to think carefully about the dangers of a proliferation of different books and pieces of paper. Anglicanism typically presupposes a middle class culture in which people are used to the printed word but in many parishes such a culture simply does not exist. Expecting members of a congregation (especially if some are elderly or disabled) to juggle with a service booklet, a hymn book and a weekly pew sheet is a large enough demand on many people and so this should be an absolute maximum.

Future developments?

Perhaps the days are coming (indeed, in some places they are already here) when it will be possible for the entire service to be electronically transmitted onto small and elegant screens (placed, for example, on pillars around a church) so that books will no longer be necessary. This would have the added advantage that the sound waves that people produce from speaking and singing would not, as they normally do now, travel downwards and hit the book but, rather, be projected outwards in a livelier and more vibrant sound. In some churches, of course, overhead projectors are used for precisely these reasons. And while OHPs generally detract from a liturgical space, large numbers of books have many problems as well.

The Chair and Altar Books

In addition to thinking about the books that are given to members of the congregation, it is also important to think a bit about the book that the president uses at the chair and (if it is different) the book that is placed on the altar.

Like everything else that is used in the Eucharist, these books need to be attractive and of good quality. Sadly, the enormous altar book published with *Common Worship* is unwieldy and difficult to use, so in practice most churches will probably want to print out material from the available resources and make their own altar book. Obviously, care is needed about the choice of books, both of which will be prominent during the service. Anything looking like a ring binder will be unattractive and out of keeping. Probably the best option is a display book with plastic pages into which sheets of A4 paper can be inserted. These books vary a great deal in quality, however, and the cheaper type will indeed look cheap. Some of them, however, are reasonably attractive and some have an insert in the front cover into which, for example, a reproduction of an icon might be placed. It will be better still if someone is able to make a suitable fabric cover to go over it.

Whatever the type of book(s) used, it is helpful for *all* the words the president needs to be included in them in an order that is easy to follow. Shuffling between different books and pieces of paper will inevitably be a distraction.

Lectionary

A large and substantial lectionary or lectern Bible is necessary as a symbol of the importance of the word in the Eucharist. In order to convey the sense of the shared nature of the

Scriptures in the Christian community, it is important that this lectionary/Bible should be read from and that readings should not be done from people's own Bibles or printed sheets.

Further guidance is given in the next chapter on the subject of the selection and delivery of scriptural readings.

Gospel Book

The reading of the gospel and not the sermon is the highlight of the Liturgy of the Word. Recent liturgical thinking has very much emphasized the importance having a gospel book that is different to the main lectionary, as a visible sign of the gospel. A large and attractive gospel book can be carried into church at the start of the service, particularly when there is a deacon. There are some very attractive gospel books in the *Common Worship* series.

Questions for Reflection and Discussion

- What are the main difficulties that people encounter in following the service in your church?
- How attractive and user-friendly are the service books?
- What type of revision might be helpful?
- How could the book of the Gospels be made more prominent so as to emphasize this most important of scriptural readings?

5

Readings

In the Anglican tradition, the Eucharist is a 'balanced' service of word and sacrament. The reading of Scripture thus has a place of the utmost importance. In chapter 11, the importance of a permanent, visual focus for the word is emphasized. In this chapter, some suggestions are offered about the selection of readings and the business of actually reading them.

How are the Readings Chosen?

Selection

In the last twenty-five years, there has been a proliferation of different lectionaries. A Church of England parish church today might use the Prayer Book lectionary for the Eucharist or the Revised Common Lectionary (RCL, with either 'continuous' or 'related' Old Testament readings) or the Roman lectionary (from which the RCL is largely derived) or the Joint Liturgical Group four-year lectionary or the, now superseded, *Alternative Service Book* lectionary.

Quite a few churches use no lectionary at all and instead devise series of sermons on individual books of the Bible with titles such as 'Amos, Man for Today'. In the view of the authors of this book, this is a regrettable development. The division and discord that is experienced in present day Anglicanism would, we think, be considerably reduced if all worshipping communities were committed to reading and reflecting on the same scriptural texts each week in their Sunday worship. The same could, of course, be said on an ecumenical level, which is why it seems unfortunate that the need was felt to make alterations to the Roman Catholic three-year lectionary in order to produce the Revised Common Lectionary. Surely it would have been a positive ecumenical gesture towards the Roman Catholic Church, and the other churches (including some Anglican ones) that only use the Roman lectionary, to have adopted this as our own. Had we done so, then we would not have the dizzyingly pluriform situation that we now experience and would have a more obviously 'shared' approach to Scripture among Christians of different kinds.

However, this has now been done and, in practice, it means that most Anglican churches will use the Revised Common Lectionary. It is an enormous relief that the new lectionary does not have, as the *ASB* did, lectionary readings constructed around pre-determined, artificially constructed 'themes', some of which lacked linguistic elegance, theological value and, indeed, any clear sense (for example, 'The Freedom of the Sons of God/The Church's Mission to the Individual'). Instead, the new lectionary enables the gospel and New Testament readings to be read in sequence as they actually occur in the Bible, giving Old Testament readings that relate to the gospel (or, on the other 'track', Old Testament readings that are, also, continuous).

Number and length of readings

Because we no longer live in an aural culture, in which listening to people read comes easily to us, many churches will feel a strong temptation to reduce the number of readings at the Sunday Eucharist from three to two (as it is in the weekday lectionary). However, there are important theological reasons for retaining the fullness of scriptural witness that the three readings (plus psalm) embody.

However, when it comes to the length of the readings, the

situation is rather different. Over-long readings often prove indigestible for congregations and can disrupt the flow of the liturgy.

So, in general, it seems best to have all three readings but possibly to use the shorter versions whenever there is an option.

How are the Readings Read?

Style of reading

As with all other tasks in the liturgy, readers need to be properly selected and trained for their task.

As well as being able to read accurately and with sensitivity to the genre of biblical material, the most important thing is that readers should:

- be able to project their voices and to a certain extent their faces and bodies outwards so as to 'connect' with the congregation. In order for this to be done, training may well be needed on use of the voice, eye contact, posture etc. Appropriate projection will not, of course, have the effect of turning the reading into a great theatrical performance since this will have the adverse effect of drawing attention to the reader rather than to the reading.

- appear to be what is called in French *engagé*, in other words excited, interested, caught up in the proclamation of God's Word to the worshipping community. Such enthusiasm will hopefully be infectious so that other members of the community are caught up in the Word of God as it is spoken through the Scriptures and are more able to understand the relevance that this has for their lives.

Following along

We have already noted that we live in a culture that does not find it easy to listen and, because of this, many churches will want to provide some means by which members of the congregation can follow the readings. It is probably best to do this in the form of a sheet, with the readings printed on it. The drawback of this, however, is that an unfortunate liturgical effect is created when, for example, the gospel is proclaimed and everyone is looking at a piece of paper rather than the gospel reader. However, having the readings printed out has the advantage that they can be taken home and, hopefully, re-read or, indeed, become the basis of a study group, formed to look closely at the readings or discuss the sermon. It is also helpful for those who do not have English as their first language. Illustrations on a service sheet can also be a helpful enhancement.

Some churches provide 'pew Bibles' but the flow of the liturgy is likely to be disrupted by readings being looked up. A printed sheet, now easy to produce or download, is likely to be preferable and can normally be combined with the parish news sheet.

Announcing

As with all announcements in the Eucharist, these need to be kept as brief and simple as possible. In particular, it is quite unnecessary to:

- Emphasize the numerical order of the readings by saying, for example, 'the *first* reading' or 'the *second* reading is from ...' It is quite obvious to most people whether a particular reading is the first or second they have heard.

- Give full chapter and verse, by saying, for example, 'The reading is taken from the first chapter of the second letter of St Paul to the Corinthians, beginning at verse eight'. The division of the Bible into chapters and verses is a convenient way of looking things up but it is not inherently important to the reading. If they are needed, they can be printed out elsewhere.

By far the best way for readings to be announced is a simple and elegant sentence such as:

'A reading from the prophet Isaiah.'

or

'A reading from the second letter of Paul to the Corinthians.'

Amplification

Like the president, readers may benefit from having their voices amplified. It is outside the scope of this book to comment on different systems of amplification but it is worth noting that no amount of amplification will compensate for a reader's poor voice projection or lack of engagement with the scriptural text.

Teaching Point

Reading the whole of God's word

The second-century heretic Marcion (d.160) argued that the God portrayed in the Old Testament was vengeful, capricious and legalistic and could not be identified with the God and Father of Jesus Christ. Thus, Marcion argued that Christians should dispense with the Hebrew Scriptures altogether as well as large sections of the New Testament. The belief has a number of striking theological problems, not least that Jesus himself clearly looks to the Old Testament on a great many occasions. In addition, dispensing with the Old Testament inevitably downplays God's role as creator, as it is described in Genesis. This, in turn pays into 'Gnostic' and dualistic views that understand the created world, including the environment and the body, as evil and thus are in conflict with a faith that takes creation and incarnation seriously.

Judging by the small number of sermons that are preached on the Old Testament and the number of people who continue to say things like 'the Old Testament God is a God of vengeance but the New Testament God is a God of love', Marcion's influence is still very much with us.

Questions for Reflection and Discussion

- Which lectionary is used in your church? Why is it used? And does it need to be changed?
- Are there materials to enable the congregation to follow the readings and, if not, should there be or is it best just to listen?
- How are potential readers selected and how well are they trained and supported?
- How adequate is the sound system (if there is one) in your church?

6

The Sermon

In many Anglican churches of the broadly catholic tradition, it has often been thought that the sermon is not particularly important. This is a seriously mistaken view, out of keeping with both Scripture and the Church's tradition and disastrous also in practical terms. In many churches, consistently poor preaching over many years has been one of the greatest single factors leading to a drop in congregational numbers. Churches of an evangelical tradition rightly see the sermon as a crucial part of the service but it is often so long that it completely overbalances the service.

In today's Church, good, thoughtful and carefully prepared sermons are increasingly important and this section will try to present some suggestions for preaching in a way that takes the sermon very seriously but, at the same time, makes it an integral part of the liturgy.

Some vital considerations for sermons at the Eucharist is that they should be:

Structured

An obvious initial point is that, like any prose composition, a sermon needs a structure. Sadly, many sermons completely lose their audiences by being rambling and inchoate without any sense of clear purpose or direction.

A good sermon will have a clear structure and this will include:

- A beginning, in which the preacher engages the congregation and introduces what is going to be said.
- A middle, the real content.
- An end, which sums up what has been said and finishes off in a reasonably powerful way so that the sermon does not just peter out.

A common structure, beloved of evangelicals but useful for everyone, is the three point sermon. Having three points enables the preacher to think in slightly smaller units, which can aid clarity. It also allows those who lose concentration to be able to return to the sermon relatively easily. However, although the three point sermon is useful (and could perhaps even be said to be Trinitarian) it will be annoying if it this method is used all the time. Contrary to the practice of some preachers, the three points do not need to begin with the same letter. However, a sermon that has been well structured will almost always be able to be summarized in a single sentence. If it can't be, then something has probably gone wrong at the planning stage.

Scriptural

The structure of *Common Worship* Order One makes it clear that the sermon forms an integral part of the Liturgy of the Word, coming after the readings and the gospel. As such, it needs to relate in an obvious way to at least one of the readings, normally, but not necessarily, the gospel. It is very tempting for preachers to make the sermon an opportunity to tell stories or talk about their favourite subjects but this, unless relevant to the readings, is an abuse of the Liturgy of the Word and needs to be resisted.

- Many congregations find the Bible bemusing and bewildering. The sermon at the Parish Eucharist will never be enough to tackle this deep-seated problem and in every parish, other strategies (for example, Bible study groups) will be needed. However, the sermon does certainly present an unmissable opportunity for the worshipping community to engage with the biblical texts and the God whom they reveal. New resources for helping make the Scriptures come alive in the sermon are constantly coming onto the market. One of the most useful strategies is to look the readings up (and preferably also a commentary on them) early in the week and mull them over for several days before the sermon has to be preached. This ensures that thoughts get a chance to crystallize before pen is put to paper.

Pastoral

That the sermon is scriptural does not mean that it will fail to relate to the lives of the worshipping community. In fact, it is crucial that it does so. Preaching is in many ways a pastoral activity and preachers who have allowed themselves the time to get on to the wavelength of a community, who have listened to people's cares and concerns and reflected theologically on these in times of prayer and meditation always preach better sermons.

Some good questions for preachers to ask themselves are:

- Does the sermon relate the stories and themes in the readings in a natural and unforced way to the concerns and struggles that people have in their lives?
- Is the sermon sufficiently simple that even the least 'switched on' in the congregation will be able to derive something from it?
- Is the sermon sufficiently thoughtful that even the most intelligent members of the congregation will find something with which to engage?
- Does the sermon give people something specific to do and not just something to think about?

- Does the sermon contain some sort of prophetic element that challenges as well as reassures?
- At the end of writing the sermon: Is this really what I believe God is calling me to say to this community on this occasion?

If the answer to all these questions, or at least to some of them, is *yes*, then it will probably be a pastoral sermon.

Liturgical

There are two principles here:

A liturgical sermon goes with the flow of the liturgy

The Eucharist, when it is well celebrated, has a flow to it, a momentum, an onward movement. This momentum is destroyed when the sermon is very long (say over fifteen minutes), and it is extremely hard to recapture. (This does not mean that sermons should be very short either – they are a crucial part of the Liturgy of the Word).

A liturgical sermon relates to the liturgy

A sermon is not a little island adrift on a liturgical sea, so it is often a good idea for some of its content to pick up resonances from the rest of the liturgy. In particular, many preachers like to make a link between the sermon and the eucharistic action that will follow later on in the service. The sermon also might make some reference to other parts of the service, such as the dismissal, the gathering or the peace. Drawing explicit connections with other parts of the liturgy is important. However, the need to make liturgical connections should not become a straightjacket. Such connections are unhelpful when they seem forced or unnatural.

It is often helpful for churches to have the occasional sermon which takes the Eucharist as its theme and explains each part (obviously, this slightly conflicts with the idea of the sermon as part of the Liturgy of the Word).

Sacramental

Christians in the catholic tradition have always believed that the bread and wine of the Eucharist are sacramental in that they don't just *remind* us of Christ but, rather, he is actually present to us in them (cf. John 6.52–8). The writings of some of the Church Fathers suggest that one could say a similar thing about the sermon (and, indeed, the entire Liturgy of the Word): it doesn't just tell us *about* Christ but Christ is actually present in the word that is proclaimed and preached. As St Augustine of Hippo says, *Christus Christum praedicat* ('Christ preaches Christ'). It is difficult to suggest practical ways for drawing out the sacramentality of the Word but among them might be:

- Care over word choice: the use of language that is simple and clear but also elegant and, at times, evocative in its use of image and metaphor.
- A tone that can be either calm or impassioned but never seems bored, cynical or gratuitously 'matey'.
- Effective use of silence, both using short, natural pauses within the sermon and also, importantly, having a few moments of silence after it which are regular and which the congregation comes to expect.
- The use (though not over-use) of actions, objects, visual aids, etc., which are sacramental both by being material objects which tell of God and because Christ himself used symbols and familiar images in his own teaching.

All of these create a certain space for the Word in the Eucharist to be able to function in a sacramental way. Obviously, if Christ is present in the word that is proclaimed and preached, that is because Christ makes himself present and not because of the preacher's linguistic abilities, imagination, or sense of timing. What a preacher *can* do, however, with the word as with the sacrament, is try to help create the conditions in which that presence can be more fully realized by the community.

Questions for Reflection and Discussion

- Which sermons are particularly memorable to you (either for good or bad reasons) and why?
- What do you think are the most important characteristics of a good sermon?
- What resources for studying the Scriptures are available in your church and how might these be enhanced?

7

The Prayers of Intercession

Context in the Eucharist

Teaching Point

Praying in the Trinity

The doctrine of the Trinity is not found in an explicit form in the New Testament, although there are strong hints of it in, for example, Jesus' command to baptize all nations in the name of the Father and of the Son and of the Holy Spirit (Matt. 28.19). Reflection on such passages led the early Church to believe that God exists in three persons and one substance, Father, Son and Holy Spirit, and this doctrine has become central to the Christian faith.

Theologians through the centuries have offered a number of different ways of attempting (although it can only ever be attempting) to understand the Trinity. It is interesting to note that the later twentieth century in particular saw a revival of theological attention being given to the subject. However, as some theologians in the early Church would point out, it is perhaps not in academic words but in the Church's prayer and worship, directed to the Father, through the Son, in the power of the Holy Spirit, that we come to first-hand knowledge of this great mystery.

One of the new features of Order One of *Common Worship* is that the Eucharist starts with the President saying, 'In the Name of the Father and of the Son and of the Holy Spirit', or, at least, the rubric says in a somewhat Anglican fashion that the President *may* say these words. They are in fact extremely important because they draw attention to a vital aspect of the Eucharist, which is that the whole service is a prayer and not simply those bits that are explicitly called prayers.

One of the recurring features of this book is the advice to those responsible for planning and leading the Eucharist to keep to an *absolute minimum* announcements such as (from former days) 'We start our service on page 119 of the *Alternative Service Book*' or 'We will now say form (b) of the Confession' or 'We will now sing hymn 487'. The reason for minimizing such announcements is not just an aesthetic one to do with choreography – although there is nothing wrong *per se* about good choreography. The main reason for avoiding too many announcements is that they puncture the sense that the Eucharistic liturgy – hymns, readings, sermon, dismissal, the lot – is a prayer from beginning to end. This does *not* mean that it needs to be celebrated with unbending seriousness and formality: God does not require that of us either in prayer or in life. What it does mean is that all words, symbols and gestures must be in some way worthy of being gathered up into the single, sustained prayer of thanksgiving that God's people offer to the triune God.

The reason why this is relevant to a chapter on Prayers of Intercession is that when people forget that the entire Eucharist is a prayer, not only can the atmosphere of certain parts of the service become very *un*-prayerful but also the part that is perhaps most obviously to do with what people think of as prayer (the intercessions) becomes overloaded: hence the normal problem with intercessions, which is that they are generally much too long. It is almost as if people are saying: 'If this is the only part of the service in which we are really going to pray, we had better do it for a good long time.'

Within the total prayer of the Eucharist, the Prayers of

Intercession exist simply to focus the prayers of the congregation in the light of their hearing of God's word in Scripture and as they prepare to participate in the sacrament. There is, of course, a time for extended intercession but this is not it. So, the vital points about intercessions are that they should be brief, simple and, if at all possible, led by a lay person.

Style and Structure

Structure

Common Worship suggests the following headings under which the intercessions can be structured:

a. The Church of Christ
b. Creation, human society, the sovereign, those in authority
c. The local community
d. Those who suffer
e. The communion of saints

This is a very helpful guide. General catholic practice would be to pray for the bishop in the prayers for the Church. Perhaps only staunch Erastians would wish to pray for the sovereign at every Eucharist. And the final one of these five headings is somewhat coy about the practice of offering prayers for the departed: an ancient element in the Christian Eucharist and, pastorally, an extremely important one.

Moving from the general to the particular

One usual complaint about intercessions is that, in praying for anything and everything (*peace throughout the world, justice for all people, the end of hunger and disease,* etc.) they are evacuated of meaningful content. Another is that they can be so specific and, in the narrow sense, parochial that they seem inward-looking or trivial ('We pray for more helpers on the cake stall at the bazaar', etc.). A good way of avoiding both of these pitfalls is to move from the general to the particular, setting particular needs and concerns within a wider framework. For example, 'We pray for all who live in poverty and want, and for those who help and support them, especially for the work of the local shelter for the homeless.'

Relevance to readings and theme

In order to give a sense of the Eucharist being a unity, it is important that the person leading the intercessions looks up the readings and tries to relate the prayers to them and to the theme (or 'intention') of the service, if there is one.

Style of language

The intercessions should be written in a style that is elegant but simple, natural and unaffected. This is not an occasion for writing poetry or expressing highly sophisticated theological thoughts. It is also not a time for a party political broadcast either to the Church or the nation, nor is it a time for intercessors to show that they are in touch with popular culture.

Consistency

A couple of small pitfalls to watch out for here:

- *Consistency of address*. It is normally a good idea for intercessions to begin in a first person plural form (for example, *Let us pray for the Church and the world* ... or *Let us pray to the Father through Jesus his son* ...). Thereafter, they can carry on addressing God indirectly (*We pray that God will bless our families and friends* ...) or directly (*Lord, we pray that you will bless our families and friends* ...). What doesn't sound good is when the two are mixed, as they very often are (as in *We pray to God for our families and friends, asking that you will bless and keep them*).

- *Consistency of ending. Common Worship* has two suggestions:

    Lord, in your mercy/Hear our prayer.

and

    Lord, hear us/Lord, graciously hear us.

Whether it is one of these or another, it needs to be clear what people are expected to say and the form should then be consistently maintained.

Brevity

The importance of the intercessions being fairly short has already been emphasized. Some hints about how to keep them brief are:

- Keep each section down to one or two sentences – no more.
- Don't incorporate longer prayers, such as the prayer of St Francis or the Mothers' Union Prayer; however good these prayers may be in other settings, they will disrupt the flow of the intercessions and the liturgy more generally.
- Regularly prune lists of the sick, departed and anniversaries. Endless lists of names will not enhance the intercessions.

Silence

It is important that the intercessions, like other parts of the Eucharist, do not become a constant gabble of words. Silence should play a vital role in them. In fact, it is in the silent pauses that people are actually able to pray for the things they are being asked to pray for before each petition is gathered up in, for example, 'Lord, in your mercy/Hear our prayer.' Each section, then, has a three-fold structure:

- Bidding (what we are praying for).
- Short period of silence (so we can pray for it).
- Response (asking God to hear the prayer we offer).

Resources

There are plenty of intercessions available to be drawn on in different liturgical books but it is almost always better not to use them. A few simple biddings, written by a member of the congregation, laying the needs of God's people before him with awareness of their particular context will almost always be better than the longer, prefabricated prayers written by liturgical experts.

Intercession and thanksgiving

A final point is that the Eucharistic Prayer is the great prayer of thanksgiving as its name suggests. This has two implications:

- The intercessions are essentially a time for 'supplication' and not for thanksgiving.
- Ways can be found of incorporating particular thanks-givings into the Eucharistic Prayer. One way of doing this is to *ad-lib* part of the preface, as was the custom in parts of the early Church.

Who leads them?

Leading the intercessions is not a presidential ministry and, where this is at all possible, this should be done by the deacon or a lay person. Having said this, of course, in some parishes it is very difficult to find a lay person with the confidence to write intercessions and it may therefore be that, for a while, one of the clergy will need to write intercessions for someone else to read out as he or she grows in confidence. Moreover, in any parish, there will need to be proper training for those writing intercessions in order to instil good practice. If it is expected that the Prayers of Intercession are brief and simple, as it is suggested here they should be, it will be much easier for a variety of lay people to feel empowered to take on this ministry.

While leading the intercessions is a lay ministry, it is appropriate for the president (sometimes at any rate) to introduce and end them since this incorporates them more naturally into the total liturgical offering. *Common Worship* provides a variety of collects and endings for intercessions that can be used for this purpose. Otherwise, such prayers can be *ad-libbed*.

Further Suggestions for the Intercessions

At different times, it may be helpful to introduce different styles for the intercessions, for example:

- The use of music, perhaps a simple verse or chant repeated after each petition.
- A group of people leading them rather than just a single individual.
- Writing out intercessions and collecting them in a basket to be offered at the offertory.
- Free prayer (if the congregation is small enough).

Questions for Reflection and Discussion

- Richard Giles (*Re-Pitching the Tent*, p. xiii) describes the intercessions as 'the most dreaded of liturgical tortures'. Do you agree?

- Which ways of leading the intercessions seem to you to be most helpful?
- What opportunities does your church have for meditative and/or intercessory prayer at other times of the week?

Teaching Point

Justin Martyr

St Justin Martyr (c.100 – c.165) was one of the early 'Apologists' who, in the early days of the Church, attempted to give an account of Christian faith and practice to authorities in the Roman Empire, in the hope of avoiding persecution. Justin's first Apology, addressed to the Roman Emperor Antonius Pius in the year 155, includes one of the first accounts that we have (possibly *the* first) of the celebration of the Eucharist after the New Testament. Justin's aim, in part, is to refute accusations of cannibalism and other unpleasant practices that were ascribed to those who claimed to consume Christ's flesh and blood in the Eucharist.

Justin's account of the Eucharist has been enormously influential for modern liturgical scholarship and has helped to refresh thinking about the way in which it is celebrated in all the denominations. In a few sentences, Justin outlines a rite of dignity and simplicity and suggests the basic structure of gathering, Liturgy of the Word, Liturgy of the Sacrament and dismissal that are fundamental to much modern liturgical thinking. Among other things, Justin particularly emphasizes the importance of the sermon, standing for the intercessions, the kiss of peace, the *mixed* chalice (that is, containing both water and wine), the Great Amen and the consecrated bread and wine being taken to those who are sick.

Part 3

Music

8

Music at the Eucharist

Liturgy is drama. And good liturgy draws the people of God into the drama so as to effect change in the lives of individuals, and to remould us in the image of Christ. Of course we are not always so renewed. When one of the authors of this book was a parish priest in London's King's Cross, one of the old faithful used to say, 'Father, why is it that people coming to church look like they are on their way to the dentist and when they go home they look like they have been?' As in good theatre we know our services have been successful when the outside kind of truth has become the inside kind of truth, truth that we can live by.

Music, perhaps more than anything else, has the power to bring emotion into our worship and it is an essential part of the Church's prayer. St Augustine of Hippo famously remarked that 'whoever sings prays twice'. The movement of the liturgy draws us deeper into the mystery of Christ's redeeming love, and brings us back again so that with renewed confidence we can go about our apostolic work. In Romans 15.16, St Paul reinforces this idea as he speaks of his calling as 'a minister [*leitourgon*] of Christ Jesus to the Gentiles in the priestly service [*hierourgounta*] of the gospel of God, so that the offering of the Gentiles may be acceptable, sanctified by the Holy Spirit'.

Different churches have widely differing musical resources. Some churches have marvellously competent choirs and organists; others have difficulty finding anyone with any instrumental or vocal skills at all. Whatever the situation, it is

necessary for those responsible for worship to take a regular
look at their music and assess how well it contributes to the
total liturgical offering of the Eucharist. Here are some suggestions for churches with different types of musical resources.

Churches with Greater Musical Resources

Churches that have a good organist and an enthusiastic and
able choir have a very great gift which, if used well, will enormously enhance their sung celebrations of the Eucharist.
However, they may still need to ask some fundamental questions. These questions relate to:

Participation of the congregation

Does the input from the musicians assist or impede the participation of the whole congregation in the Eucharist? A good
choir, organist and choir director can aid such participation
but it is also possible for the excellence of the choir actually to
impede the rest of the congregation from musical participation in the liturgy. If this is happening, strategies need to be
put in place to enable the choir to act as 'leaven in the lump',
aiding rather than dominating the singing of the entire congregation. One such strategy might be the relocation of the
choir stalls which, in their usual position – in the chancel
removed from the rest of the congregation and at ninety
degrees to it – can rarely help to enhance singing and also act
as a barrier between the rest of the congregation and the altar
(see chapter 11).

Relation to the liturgy

Does the music fit with the liturgy? In many churches, the
choir gives the appearance of doing its own thing, singing its
own hymns and anthems in a way that is disconnected from
the rest of what is happening in the service. Similarly, good

organists sometimes like to use some part of the Eucharist for a performance highlighting their musical skills. The best liturgical music will fit so well with the liturgy that the two become a seamless unity. The best choirs and organists become, in a sense, invisible since all their efforts are taken up into the total liturgical offering.

Churches with Fewer Musical Resources

Some suggestions for churches where music is a struggle:

Go for simplicity

Some music is better than no music. Occasionally, when time and resources are restricted, it is necessary to be very selective about what is sung and what is said but it is almost always possible to sing something. In the context of the Eucharist, with its emphasis on Word and Sacrament, strictly speaking the two most important parts to sing are the Alleluia Chant (to greet the gospel) and a hymn or song at the offertory (when the bread and wine are prepared on the altar). Once these are established, it is possible to build on them. Other suggestions for simple musical touches might be to play some music over the church sound system before and after the service and at the communion, or a recording of an organ voluntary at the end, or to ask a single guitar player to accompany a said Eucharistic Prayer with a succession of chords – the effect these simple things have can be amazing.

Think about employing a cantor

In the Catholic Church on the Continent, many churches enlist the services of an 'animator' whose role is to enliven the singing and make the congregation feel more secure by giving a strong vocal lead. This person will often act as the cantor as well and may, in addition, indicate the rise and fall of congregational musical phrases by appropriate hand gestures. In services both great and small, in crowded cathedrals and in 'normal' parish churches, this can greatly enhance the willingness of the congregation to join in. It is certainly best if cantors, like all musicians, are drawn into the collaborative way the liturgy is planned at an early stage. They also need to be people who are participating in the worship. If there is no one in the congregation who can act as a cantor, it may be that there is a local church with a large choir or music group which would be willing to spare a member or members to help in a parish where music is more difficult.

Don't feel tied to the organ

The organ is a marvellous instrument of extraordinary range and power which enhances the worship of many churches. However, there is no biblical injunction that liturgical music needs always to be accompanied by the organ. Indeed, in churches with small congregations, the organ can, especially if it is not played sensitively, drown the singing and thus impede musical participation in the liturgy. Nowadays, it is less and less easy to find competent organists and so the time has come for many churches to take a bit of a step of faith and to use people who are competent on other instruments. Pianos, guitars and flutes are all versatile instruments which can greatly assist congregational singing.

Find ways to introduce new music

If there is not much confidence about singing, it might be a good idea for the congregation to have a short music practice before the Eucharist begins or perhaps have a weekday evening slot set aside for this. Other ideas might be an occasional hymn-singing evening, accompanied by food and wine or a 'Songs of Praise style' service where people can vote for their favourites beforehand – and perhaps a couple of others can also be slipped in. It is surprising how popular such events often are. It is, of course, important not to overload people. A good general rule for introducing new music is never to introduce more than one new item in a particular service and then always repeat it the next week.

Consider starting a music group

Many people very much enjoy singing and so, even in quite small congregations, it may be possible to form a group who sit together in church and boost the overall quality of the singing, perhaps singing something simple themselves at some point. Having said this, it is probably the case that no choir is better than a bad choir.

Two Final Musical Points

Ancient and modern

New music both for hymns and Mass settings is always coming on the market. Sometimes, for rather snobbish reasons, people can be extremely reluctant to sing it. It often does not seem to dawn on people that even *Praise my Soul, the King of Heaven* was a new hymn once. It is only by being ready to sing new material that the Church can fulfil an important duty to future generations of sifting the good from the bad, so as to know what we can hand on. Most of the new hymn books now coming on to the market have a reasonable selection of modern hymns and in most parishes a mixture of traditional and more contemporary hymns will work best (cf. Matt. 13.52). A congregation will be kept musically fresh if new items are regularly introduced.

Musical quality

In past centuries, so far as music and drama were concerned, the Eucharist was the only show in town, the only place in which most people could experience these things for them-

selves. Today, of course, our access to music and drama is very
much greater. The inevitable result of being able to switch on
a CD player and hear the choir of King's College Cambridge is
that, however good a church congregation sounds, it will seem
somewhat ropey by comparison. This is where it is very important to remember a point loved by the fifth century bishop,
Augustine of Hippo, that God hears the voices of our hearts
and not just our lips. This book is written out of a conviction
that every effort should be made to ensure that parish liturgy
is of the highest possible standard. However, combined with
this aim needs to come the realistic insight that God does
indeed hear what is in our hearts and that a small group of
people doing their utmost to make a joyful noise in praise of
him is ultimately more valuable than the most perfect choir or
orchestra whose heart is not in it. Having done all we can to
ensure good and appropriate music at the Eucharist, we need
to be able to rest securely in that knowledge.

Questions for Reflection and Discussion

- Has your church got greater or lesser musical resources?
  List what makes you think this.
- How well are the existing musical resources used and how
  might they be developed?
- What helps people to sing well in your church and what
  hinders them?
- How open is your church to new music being introduced?

9

Hymns and Songs

The remainder of this section will make a distinction between the hymns sung at the Eucharist (covered in this chapter) and the Mass setting (covered in the next one). This distinction is convenient, since it is the one made in most churches. It is, however, not entirely helpful since some parts of the Eucharist (such as the Alleluia or the Great Amen) do not easily fit into either category. It is, further, to be hoped that in the Church of the future, rather than distinguishing between hymns and setting, the question will simply be asked which music fits best with each part of the liturgy? This chapter aims to give some guidelines on the first of these subjects in order to help choose hymns that, in a sung celebration, will fit easily and appropriately into the total liturgical offering.

Principles of Hymn Choice

Two basic principles for hymns and songs during the Eucharist are that they should be liturgically appropriate and thematically appropriate.

Liturgically appropriate

In chapter 8, we stressed the power of music to bring emotion into worship. In a recent book entitled *Secularisation* (Continuum, London and New York, 2002), Edward Norman argues that, whereas worship in the past was understood as something done in order to honour God, nowadays its main point seems to be to make people feel better. This view is an over-simplification. To be sure, the main point of worship is to honour God but it has also always been the case in the Jewish and Christian traditions that this process has had an 'affective' dimension to it: involving worshippers on the level of feeling and emotion to which music is integrally related, so that we can sing with the Psalmist, 'Make a joyful noise to the Lord, all the earth. Worship the Lord with gladness' (Ps. 100.1–2).

Part of achieving liturgical appropriateness is ensuring that the hymns and songs that are chosen fit with the emotion that is generated by different sections of the liturgy. Some hymns are good for gathering, others for offering, some for contemplation and adoration, and some for sending out. Mix them up and you mix your messages, and mixed messages always create confusion and conflict.

For example, it is not appropriate to start a service with *Bread of heaven on thee we feed* because a hymn like that is the perfect musical expression of the encounter of the hungry soul with the bread of life: it has an intimate, meditative feel that makes it suitable to be a communion hymn. Similarly it would not work to sing *Christ triumphant, ever reigning* at the moment of receiving communion because it is an upbeat, sending out type of song, appropriate for the dismissal.

It is amazing how often this fundamental point is missed – music embodies emotion, and the emotion must suit the progress of the liturgy.

Thematically appropriate

Hymns that are chosen for the Eucharist obviously need not only to fit in with the liturgy and the different emotions it generates at each point but also with the theological themes that are suggested by the readings and prayers.

Getting this right is more complicated in the Revised Common Lectionary than was the case with the *ASB* lectionary where the readings were chosen to fit a predetermined theme. On the whole, this development is very welcome (see chapter 5) but it can create some difficulties when it comes to selecting suitable hymns.

There are a large number of resources available to help with choosing hymns that reflect the service's central themes.

- Most modern hymn books have suggestions about which hymns to use on different Sundays of the year, bearing in mind the readings that have been set for the day. These can never be used without careful thought but they provide a useful starting point.

- Another valuable resource is that the Royal School of Church Music publishes a journal each quarter which greatly aids choosing hymns, anthems and even organ music.

- Hymnquest is also useful. An electronic resource, published by Stainer & Bell, it enables users to access texts of hymns and songs together with details of their copyright situation. These can then be cut and pasted into an order of service. Hymnquest also makes it possible to look up hymns that contain particular scriptural echoes, or are relevant to particular themes.

Most of all, it is important that clergy, choir directors and others responsible for church music should not be afraid to use their own creative skills. It is particularly useful to keep a notebook in which to note down hymns that seem to fit in with particular seasons, festivals or points in the Eucharist. (It is also a good idea to note down which have been used so as to avoid over-frequent repetition.)

Practical Guidance on Hymn Choice

Bearing in mind these two guiding principles, here are some more specific suggestions about which type of hymns work at different points in the Eucharist.

Entrance hymn

The entrance hymn needs to be reasonably long in order to ensure that clergy, servers (and choir) have enough time to leave the vestry and reach their places in the sanctuary – although not so long that by the time this has happened there are still many verses to be sung. Since it comes right at the start of the service, it should aim to be fairly familiar to members of the congregation because its function is to gather the people, to get them involved as participants, not to make them feel like passive observers!

Psalm

Common Worship lays a greater emphasis than did the *ASB* on the importance of having a psalm between the first two readings as a response to the Old Testament reading. However, the psalm certainly need not be sung, and if it cannot be sung well, it might be best not to try. It can be recited by one voice, recited by everyone or said verse by verse antiphonally. In churches lucky enough to have a competent singer who is prepared to act as a cantor, the psalm can be sung responsorially, and there are several collections of such settings. It can also be sung to a simplified Anglican chant or using versions in books such as *Psalm Praise*. There is of course no reason why the way in which the psalm is said or sung cannot vary from week to week.

Alleluia (gospel acclamation)

Teaching Point

The alleluia

The alleluia (NB pronounced as it is spelt and not, as is sometimes heard, *allelulia*) comes from Hebrew and means literally 'praise ye the Lord'. In the Psalms and elsewhere in the Bible, it expresses joyful praise. Because of this, it came to be associated in Christian usage with the season of Easter and rejoicing at the resurrection of Christ. (In the Western Church, during the penitential season of Lent, there are traditionally no alleluias).

In the Eucharist, an alleluia chant is also traditionally used to greet the gospel, again expressing joy in the good news that Christ brings. This ancient part of the liturgy is finding a new home in Anglican services, which increasingly suggest its use.

The monastic settings in the *Graduale Romanum* are elaborate and very beautiful, beyond the ability of an ordinary congregation but within the range of a competent choir with a few strong voices. Another alternative is to use one of the simpler tones by composers such as Gelineau or Inwood. There are also some simple and powerful congregational alleluias, like the Celtic Alleluia or those devised by the Taizé community – both of which are effective so long as they are not overused. Whatever the case, the gospel acclamation, incorporating, as it does, a sentence from the gospel of the day, is one of the most important liturgical links. Less familiar than many hymns, it will need to be practised before the service if it is not already known.

Gradual hymn?

Because *Common Worship* restores the psalm and the alleluia to their original importance in the liturgy, there is essentially no reason to retain what used to be called the gradual hymn, which was itself originally a psalm, or portion of a psalm. Concentrating on the psalm and the alleluia will create a much better liturgical flow. In some churches, affection for the gradual hymn will make it difficult to dispense with. If this is the

case, it needs to be short and, if possible, reflect the readings.
There should *not* be both a gradual hymn and an alleluia.

Offertory hymn

Quite a wide variety of hymns are suitable for the offertory.
One of the main criteria is that the offertory hymn should be
long enough to cover the preparation of bread and wine on the
altar and anything else that needs to be done (such as censing
the gifts). If the hymn finishes while these things are still happening, it is always best for some music to continue (without
singing) in order to avoid an awkward 'pregnant pause'. It
might also be a good idea for the offertory hymn to be one that
picks up any particular themes from the readings as a sort of
bridge between the Liturgy of the Word and the Liturgy of the
Sacrament.

Communion hymn

It has already been pointed out that the communion hymn
comes at a profound moment in the service, after or during the
time that people are receiving communion. It is thus appropriate for it to have a meditative feel so as to make it a helpful aid
to devotion. In view of its place in the service, hymns and songs
with some sort of eucharistic connection (even if this is quite
tenuous) are appropriate at this point.

Final hymn

In *Common Worship* there is a difference between the nature
of the post-communion prayer said by the president, and the
prayer of thanksgiving which is said by the whole congregation
together. The president's prayer completes the communion rite
and appropriately concludes a period of silence after people
have received. By contrast, the congregational prayers are all
centred on the theme of being sent out. For this reason there is

a strong argument for inserting the final hymn *between* these two post-communion prayers.

Alternatively, the final hymn can be a 'recessional' hymn although there are quite strong liturgical arguments against a hymn being sung after the dismissal (when people are told to 'Go in peace to love and serve the Lord', should they then be remaining to sing a hymn?).

Whichever position is chosen, the final hymn normally needs to be something thankful, confident, uplifting – it's a tough old world out there and the right choice of hymn at this point helps give the congregation some confidence that the Eucharist has equipped them to face it.

Questions for Reflection and Discussion

• Which hymns or songs are sung best in your church and why?
• Which hymns/songs are sung worst and why?
• Think about the way the Eucharist is structured. Which hymns/songs fit in well with different parts of the service?
• Which hymns/songs seem to fit in well with different seasons of the Church's year?

The Mass Setting

In addition to the hymns, a number of other parts of the Eucharist are very often sung. These are, in the Liturgy of the Word:

* Kyrie Eleison (Lord, have mercy).

* Gloria in Excelsis (Glory to God in the highest).

and in the Liturgy of the Sacrament:

* Sanctus (Holy, Holy, Holy).

* Benedictus (Blessed is he ...).

* Eucharistic Acclamation (Christ has died ... etc.).

* The Great Amen at the end of the Eucharistic Prayer.

* In some churches, the Lord's Prayer, sung to a simple chant.

* Agnus Dei (Lamb of God ...).

There are so many settings of these available that even churches with very few musical resources will find it comparatively easy to sing a variety of settings over the course of the year. In addition to the resources already mentioned, a very helpful place to look is the liturgical section of the *Celebration Hymnal for Everyone* (McCrimmons, Great Wakering, Essex, 1994), which contains a large number of different settings that can, to an extent, be mixed and matched.

Taking a Closer Look

Kyrie Eleison

Common Worship strongly suggests that the Kyrie Eleison belongs within the Prayers of Penitence and not after them. This makes very good liturgical sense, bearing in mind the words of the Kyrie. The Kyrie can be sung by the whole congregation but its nature also makes it suitable for singing meditatively by the choir or a soloist. Sung 'penitential' Kyries in which a short sentence is sung before each of the three parts, replacing longer prayers of confession, can also be very effective.

Gloria

In contrast to the Kyrie, the Gloria is a text which, even when there is a good choir, definitely suits congregational participation. The Gloria is a joyful shout of praise (although at many churches you would never know this) and so it properly belongs to the people. An unsatisfactory element in some cathedral worship is that the elaborate settings of the Gloria so beloved by musicians, and so accomplished in their musical range, leave the congregation feeling left out and disenfranchised.

The main problem with singing the Gloria, of course, is that it is so much longer than the other sung texts and so it can be a struggle to teach it to unconfident singers. If a congregation can't make this a joyful noise unto the Lord, there are a variety of responsorial versions, such as the Lourdes Gloria or the 'clap' Gloria by Mike Anderson which will make it much easier. If all else fails, say or shout it out together!

Sanctus

As with the Gloria, the Sanctus calls for a *congregational* setting. The logic of the Eucharistic Prayer strongly suggests that

it belongs to the people of God to join with the whole company of angels and archangels in their song of praise: *Holy,
Holy, Holy*. It also needs to flow immediately on from the pre-
ceding words in the Eucharistic Prayer, which announce it.
It sounds ridiculous when, as regrettably often happens in
choral settings, the president says, 'Therefore with angels and
archangels and with all the company of heaven we proclaim
your great and glorious name, for ever praising you and
singing ...', and the organist then takes a protracted period to
play a note for the choir, which then, after another pregnant
pause finally begins to sing!

Benedictus

The Benedictus comes immediately after the Sanctus but it is
not so strongly congregational in nature and can, therefore,
appropriately be sung by a choir or a soloist in churches where
these are available.

Eucharistic Acclamation

Common Worship gives a total of four Eucharistic Acclamations. These can be sung but do not necessarily need to be.
The acclamation expresses, at this point in the Eucharistic
Prayer, joy and confidence in Christ's redeeming work, so a
short verse that is joyful and confident in its words and music
is appropriate, perhaps even one that does not follow the
given forms in the liturgy. In one church with which the
authors are familiar, the acclamation at Midnight Mass on
Christmas Eve is the verse of *O Come all ye Faithful* that starts
Yea, Lord, we greet thee, born this happy morning.

The Great Amen*

The Great Amen at the end of the Eucharistic Prayer is not traditionally part of the Mass setting but it is a vital and often

---

* See Teaching Point on page 4.

neglected part of the Eucharist. The early Christian writer Justin Martyr in his description of the Eucharist in AD 150 writes that 'When [the president] has concluded the prayers and thanksgivings, all the people express their joyful assent by saying Amen. (Amen in the Hebrew language means *so be it*.)' How good it would be if the Amen at the end of the Eucharistic Prayer was indeed a loud and joyful assent, instead of, as so often, a rather dull murmur. There are a variety of sung Amens that can be used to encourage this. Alternatively, congregations can be taught its significance so that they say it loudly and confidently.

Agnus Dei

The Agnus Dei, like the Kyrie and the Benedictus but unlike the Gloria and the Sanctus, is a more meditative part of the service, suited to being sung by a choir or soloist or said by the whole congregation. However the Agnus Dei is sung, it is important to remember that it comes at a very crucial point in the Eucharist and many people have remarked over the years about the importance to them of its words as a prayer of preparation before receiving the sacrament. Both of the authors of this book have experienced members of the congregation feeling cheated when, in order to save time, the Agnus Dei has been moved from being a prayer of preparation to being an anthem sung while people are receiving communion. Who wants to save time at the most profound moment of the mystery?

Two Final Points

Music and eucharistic presidency

There are various parts of the Eucharist (in particular, the collect and the Eucharistic Prayer – particularly the preface and the doxology at the end of it) which can be sung by the president. Music is provided for this in, among other places, the large hardback *Common Worship* altar book. If these texts are sung well, it can greatly enhance the Eucharist and make it more fully a *sung* celebration. If they are sung badly it can be a complete disaster, so this should only ever be contemplated by competent singers. If the collect and the preface are to be sung, they sound best when sung naturally, not as a full-blown operatic performance.

Music and the gospel

Just as the Eucharistic Prayer is sung as the highlight of the Liturgy of the Sacrament, so in some churches, the gospel is sung as the highlight of the Liturgy of the Word. Again, this should only be done by those who are very competent singers. In addition experience tends to suggest that singing the gospel distracts people from the important task of listening to its words; words which, unlike those of the Eucharistic Prayer, are not often repeated from service to service. There is, then, a strong case for saying that, in normal circumstances, the gospel should not be sung.

Part 4

Things

11

Space

Christians often describe God as being both transcendent and immanent; meaning, on the one hand, above and beyond all that we can possibly know or imagine and, on the other, intimately present to us at every moment and particularly present in the celebration of the Eucharist. Different types of worship space reflect these characteristics in different ways and to different degrees. The view that this book tries to encourage is that the Eucharist should be celebrated in a space that combines a sense of transcendence and immanence, and doesn't lose either one or the other.

For example, a large church in which the high altar is used at the east end, separated from the congregation by a very long distance, strongly reinforces a sense of God's transcendence. However, it may well convey a sense of God being remote and distant rather than immanent. By contrast, a church with a central altar that the whole congregation gathers around will be likely to give a sense of God's presence in and through the other members of the congregation but might not show much about transcendence or otherness.

There is of course a pastoral and evangelistic point here. In churches where the liturgical action seems distant and remote it will certainly be more difficult for newcomers to feel involved in the service or, in many cases, have any clue what is going on. On the other hand, churches where the congregation is closely huddled together and everyone very visible to each other may prevent those who are unsure or uncommitted from taking the first exploratory steps into worship.

This is *not* to say that high altars or central altars should never be used: both work very well in different local settings. It *is* to say that these things are not just incidental but carry strong theological messages which do need to be considered. This chapter tries to offer some suggestions for a liturgical space that will combine immanence with transcendence.

A Sense of Space

The best environment in which to celebrate the Eucharist is a simple, uncluttered space that has nothing in it apart from a few necessary pieces of furniture. Some churches, because of their height, give a sense of *vertical* space, as you look upwards. But, in addition to this, churches need to have a sense of *horizontal* space, especially in the area around the altar and lectern where the liturgy is focused. Sadly, most Anglican churches are seriously over-furnished: chopped up into pieces by an abundance of pews; full of clutter of different sorts: tables, prayer desks, flags and other bits of paraphernalia. These items tend to make church interiors visually unattractive and inflexible. Generally, they desperately need to be cleared away.

As church builders of previous generations (as well as those of today) understood, a sense of space in churches can do a great deal to foster prayerfulness and attentiveness, concentrating people's minds and hearts on God. And today the necessity is even greater since many people, particularly in city areas, live in cramped and claustrophobic environments.

In addition to this, there are some practical reasons for it: a spacious liturgical area will be easier to decorate. Arrangements of flowers or pictures or harvest gifts will look far better when set against a simple, uncluttered backdrop than they will when competing for attention with various bits of church bric-a-brac. An uncluttered space will also create flexibility and provide a better arena for, for example, a Sunday School presentation, a Nativity play, different sorts of services, even a church bazaar. Groups who might use the church for music or drama will thank you for clearing a space for their rehearsals or performances (which theatre or concert hall do you ever see cluttered with unused pieces of furniture?). Most of all, during the course of the service, people's attention will, with a spacious visual focus, more easily concentrate on the things in the Eucharist that really matter: the proclamation of the word of God in Scripture and the bread and wine of the Eucharist: taken, blessed, broken and distributed.

An Arrangement of Furniture that Suits the Liturgy

There are really only three pieces of furniture that are strictly necessary for the Eucharist: an altar, a lectern and a president's chair. When thinking about the worship space, we suggest:

- that, because of their importance in the liturgy, these be permanently in place at all times;
- that worshipping communities ask themselves whether any of the other items that may be lying around really are needed.

The most obvious thing is the *altar* or communion table. The *Book of Common Prayer* Order of Holy Communion says that this should 'stand in the body of the church' and in the vast majority of churches, that's just where it should be: in a place where members of the congregation can see it and relate to it and feel that they are participating fully in the Eucharist. For this reason, it is not desirable for the altar to be separated from the main body of the congregation by choir stalls, as is the case in many churches (this also has musical implications: see chapter 8). Wherever the altar is situated, it is important that it does not stand in a confined space but has at least, say, three feet of space all around it so as to make the movement involved in the Eucharist free and natural rather than cramped and fussy. The prominence of the altar is enhanced if it stands

alone. It is very rare that, for example, kneelers at either end
of altar rails add anything at all to a liturgical space.

The second necessary piece of furniture is a *lectern*, providing a physical focus for the word as the altar does for the
sacrament. This is in line with *Common Worship* and
Anglican liturgy generally, which envisages the Eucharist as a
balanced service of word and sacrament. In order to emphasize this, the lectern, like the altar, needs to be solid and promi-
nently placed so that the readings at the Eucharist are seen as
a central part of the service and are clearly audible. Ideally, the
lectern should be large and solid enough to store books and
other materials needed for the Liturgy of the Word so that it
becomes both a fixed symbol of the liturgy and also a practical piece of furniture. The lectern should be reasonably near
the altar (though not cramped up next to it) so as to relate
word and sacrament to one another in a natural way. It is
preferable that *all* the readings and the sermon should be done
from the same lectern, making a single obvious focus for the
whole proclamation of the word. This having been said, there
are good reasons why, for example, churches that have a pul-
pit will want this to be used for the sermon. What can almost
always be avoided (but sadly often isn't) is a proliferation of
different lecterns. One lectern is always enough if it is properly positioned.

The third piece of furniture needed in a liturgical space is a
chair for the president to sit on and to preside over the liturgy.
If, as in *Common Worship*, the altar is the focus for the
Liturgy of the Sacrament and the lectern for the Liturgy of the
Word, the chair is a focus for the other parts of the service: the
gathering at the start and the dismissal at the end. As with the
altar and the lectern, it is best for the chair to be in a prominent position either behind the altar or (preferably) to one side
of it so that the person of the president does not become too
much of a focus. The chair needs to be positioned so that the
president can preside from it (both sitting and standing) in a
natural and relaxed way, facing the congregation (perhaps at
a bit of an angle but not at ninety degrees) and without having

to bellow across too great a distance. It conveys the wrong impression about the role of the president if the chair looks much like a monarch's throne or a magistrate's bench and so the chair should not, for example, be raised up higher than the altar. Equally, however, as a focal point of the liturgy, the chair should not be moved at different points during the service. The president should not normally need a bookstand or second lectern in front of the chair to read from when standing up. This acts as a barrier between the president and the rest of the congregation. It is far better for a server to come and hold the book when necessary as this reinforces the sense that a team of people are working together in the Eucharist. If it is impossible for this to be arranged, the president can hold the book at the few times (such as the collect) when it is really necessary.

In addition, it will also probably be necessary to have a credence table, preferably situated to the right of the 'working side' of the altar on which bread, wine, etc. can be kept until they are needed. The credence table will look best if it is related to the altar in design and about a quarter of the size. It should not be so large that it dwarfs the essential pieces of furniture but it should be large enough to accommodate all that it needs to without looking overcrowded. If (in addition to the president) there is a deacon at the Eucharist, a chair or stool will need to be placed to the right of the president's chair. As with the other chairs (such as those for servers), this should be smaller than the president's chair so that the centrality of the president's chair continues to be emphasized.

Teaching Point

The chair

The bishop's chair (Latin: *cathedra*) is what gives cathedrals their name. Cathedrals are, literally, places where the bishop has his chair. In the early Church, cathedrals would often have a rounded 'apse' at the east end. In the centre of this would be the bishop's chair from which he would preside and preach. Around this chair would be benches on which the presbyters (or priests) would sit. Such an arrangement reinforced the collaborative nature of the ordained ministry.

The president's chair, which derives from that of the bishop, is thus not simply a functional piece of church furniture which can be ignored for most of the service and cleared away when it is not needed. Rather, even when the Eucharist is not going on, the chair symbolizes leadership in the community of faith (albeit a style of leadership that is supposed to have service as its principal characteristic). During the Eucharist itself, the chair is the place from which the president presides over the assembly, whether sitting down or standing: it is one of the focal points of the liturgical action.

Difficulties of Reordering the Space

In the introduction to this book, it was claimed that huge reordering schemes would not be suggested. After these comments, this may appear misleading, so perhaps it is worthwhile making two final comments.

- First of all, the type of reordering that achieves a simple, uncluttered and attractive liturgical space does not necessarily need to be very drastic. Often it can be achieved by, for example, removing (or relocating) two or three rows of pews and putting the altar, lectern and chair in the space that has been cleared.
- Second, the three essential pieces of furniture that have been described all need to be attractive, good quality and in reasonable proportion to one another. We are not, by any means, advocating a severely functional approach that pays no attention to the aesthetic. However, most churches already have furniture that will serve or indeed are serving

these purposes perfectly well. It may well be more a matter of repositioning what already exists than buying a lot of new things.

The authors realize, of course, that it is sometimes difficult to obtain permission to make even small alterations. However, the sort of changes we have suggested could be claimed to be 'reversible': they do not, necessarily, entail making the church look completely different or adding a lot of new things. They will also tend to make it easier for the church to host different types of events and thus increase its accessibility to the wider community. Furthermore, clearing space and removing unnecessary clutter also has the added advantage of facilitating disabled access: now a legal requirement.

For communities who are exploring more adventurous schemes of reordering for contemporary worship and mission (and certainly many churches do need to take radical action in this respect), Richard Giles' *Re-Pitching the Tent* (see bibliography) is an extremely helpful guide.

A Final Action List on Liturgical Space

Think outside the box

For example, are altar frontals, super-frontals, top cloths, cloth hangings, pieces of carpet, cheaply reproduced icons and pictures, etc. needed when they may be hiding a piece of glorious carving or a simple and elegant structure or window frame or piece of tiled floor? The new nave altar at Bristol Cathedral has a corporal placed directly on it. Its beauty is enhanced by the fact that it is left bare at all times when the Eucharist is not being celebrated.

Jettison clutter

A constantly reiterated theme in this chapter. A good exercise each summer is to take a look at everything and ask the question, 'Do we really need this?' Ask it about the burse and veil (both unnecessary), palls and (God forbid) maniples. What do they *really* contribute to a simple, dignified celebration that aims simply and unself-consciously to highlight the word and sacrament of the Eucharist?

Reclaim what is good

In many churches, the Liturgical Movement ushered in new fabrics, vestments and, indeed, pieces of furniture which are highly reminiscent of the 1970s. They may have been right for their time but now often look more tired and dated than items that are considerably older. In many churches beautiful and serviceable objects languish unused in the sacristy or lying around the church. These could do with being reclaimed for a renewed liturgical space.

Questions for Reflection and Discussion

- In what ways does your church building express transcendence and/or immanence?
- Does the church contain clutter that needs to be dispensed with or relocated?
- What messages are given by the current arrangement of altar, lectern and chair and how might these be enhanced?

12

Bread and Wine

The previous chapter looked at the issue of space – the way that churches (and other places) are laid out for the celebration of the Eucharist. This chapter and the next will look more closely at the things that are used within that space.

A point already made that needs reiterating: churches notoriously attract clutter. This is inevitable because churches matter to people. There are all sorts of associations, with births, marriages and deaths, with moments of change and insight. Churches resonate deeply, subliminally. And our desire is to adorn them with outward gifts that signify an inward and spiritual reality. Removing the clutter will never be easy because of all this invested meaning. Part of the challenge here is to clear the clutter in our minds: get the single message and go for it rigorously!

The removal of clutter is associated with another important theme in this book: the role of silence in worship. Thus an uncluttered liturgical space accompanies an uncluttered liturgy with plenty of silence. The sense of space and silence that this can encourage is helpful not only for its own sake but also because it helps the Christian community to cultivate the necessary listening skills for good pastoral care. The twentieth century theologian and martyr Dietrich Bonhoeffer writes: 'Many people are looking for an ear that will listen. They do not find it among Christians because these Christians are talking when they should be listening ... This is the beginning of the death of the spiritual life' (*Life Together*, SCM Press, 1954, p. 75).

Some degree of rationalization and an essential simplicity are vital if we are to be protected from sending out mixed messages. This may mean using different things at different times of year (such as a Christmas crib or an Easter garden). It may mean making the most of one object, while clearing away the rest (for example, finding a prominent place for the aumbry or tabernacle in which the sacrament is reserved and/or providing a place for people to light candles as part of their prayer).

The more detailed advice below thus suggests simple objects which have an obvious purpose and significance in the celebration of the Eucharist. It should be added that, like everything used in worship of God, they should be of the highest quality and beauty possible and kept scrupulously clean. This chapter will consider the 'essentials' of celebrating the Eucharist: bread, wine and a book on the altar. The following chapter will look at some things that are less essential but nonetheless important.

Bread

Size

Liturgists have often remarked (sadly to little effect) that the words 'We who are many are one body because we all share in one bread' make no sense if, as in most churches, small individual wafers are used for communion. The use of these may be convenient but it entirely spoils the symbolism that these words convey. Nowadays there are plenty of suppliers who can provide wafers that can be broken into as many as thirty-two pieces.

Type

The fact that the Last Supper was celebrated with unleavened bread and also the desire (out of respect for the sacrament) not to have too many crumbs being scattered around means that unleavened, flat bread is most appropriate for use at the Eucharist. However, in many churches the wafers used are small and fragile and melt in the mouth. The Greek verb that Jesus uses to describe this part of the Eucharist in the phrase 'Take, eat ...' (cf. Matt. 26.27 etc.) does not mean 'place on your tongue until it disintegrates'! It means something more like 'devour' or 'consume'. So, unleavened bread, yes, but preferably a type that is reasonably substantial so that it can indeed be devoured or consumed.

(In addition, it is important to note that for medical conditions such as coeliac disease, gluten free wafers must be available if needed).

Teaching Point

Passover

Passover is one of the major festivals of the Jewish year, celebrated in the early spring. The story of God's deliverance of his people from slavery in Egypt is retold and commemorated within the context of a communal meal (cf. Ex. 12—14). The Passover meal includes food that symbolizes the Exodus story: bitter herbs, lamb and unleavened bread. Because of possible discrepancies in the Gospels' accounts of the date of the Last Supper, scholarly opinion is divided as to whether it was or was not a Passover meal. At the very least, the supper was clearly a special fellowship meal, with connotations of the Passover. In addition to this, the New Testament authors clearly link Jesus' death with the Exodus story and the Passover (cf. Mark 10.45; Rom. 3.25). The use of unleavened bread in the Eucharist maintains this important connection with the Passover and the important themes of fellowship and liberation that are associated with it.

Wine

In the parish in which one of the authors of this book was a curate, an arrangement had been made in the 1970s between the vicar and one of the parishioners that the parishioner should supply home-brewed wine for the Eucharist. Twenty years later, the church continued to suffer every day of the week the effects of this agreement: a purple substance nauseous to the senses both of smell and taste, which, once in the chalice, often had large globules of detritus floating near its surface.

When communicants receive the blood of Christ from the chalice, it is surely right that a good quality wine that tastes pleasant should be used. As with the choice of bread, it may be that some parishes have to experiment with the exact type that they use from the available options, many of which are absolutely fine. One suggestion might be a white dessert wine (Muscat de Beaumes de Venice) throughout Eastertide, as a symbol of the blood of the Risen Christ, and red outside this Queen of the Seasons.

According to the *Book of Common Prayer* and the canons of the Church of England (B17), the wine used for the celebration of Holy Communion should *always* be fermented.

Vessels

Number

Many altars suffer from being cluttered with large numbers of objects. Ideally, there should be just one paten (of sufficient size to hold a host or hosts big enough to communicate all the people once it is broken) and one chalice for the wine. For practical reasons, however, such as larger numbers of communicants, a ciborium may be needed for extra wafers and more than one chalice for the wine. If so, it may be sensible to consecrate extra wine in a flagon – many churches have beautiful flagons – and then pour it into the necessary number of chalices during the Agnus Dei (the extra chalice[s] can be kept on the credence table during the Eucharistic Prayer and brought to the altar when they are needed). As a rule of thumb, the altar will *always* look cluttered if it has on it more than one paten, one ciborium, two chalices and a book. But it is better still to have simply one large paten, one chalice and (if necessary) a flagon.

Design

There are, of course, many different designs of patens and chalices on the market. Different types will suit different places and so it would be unwise to be too prescriptive. However, good general guidance is that liturgical items should actually resemble what they are used for. Thus, a receptacle for bread will look like a plate and not like a cup; flagons for wine and water will be full-sized jugs or bottles and will not resemble dispensers for oil and vinegar; a lavabo bowl will look like a basin in which hands can be properly washed and not like a small glass ramekin. If these things are generously proportioned, they will be able to do their symbolic work much more effectively.

For those who are looking to purchase new vessels, other key things to look for are simplicity, practicality, beauty and a style and proportion that are suitable for the worship space.

Pottery vessels which cannot be wiped clean easily are consequently less hygienic and also, of course, are liable to break.

Candles

A final 'almost-essential' for the celebration of the Eucharist in the catholic tradition is a candle or candles. Originally, in the days before electric lighting, the function of candles was practical, but they also symbolize Christ the light of the world. Candles are traditionally used to draw special attention to the

two main elements of the Eucharist: the Liturgy of the Word
and the Liturgy of the Sacrament. Although in many churches,
candles are brought in at the start of the service in an entrance
procession, their role is not, as it might seem, to highlight the
president but rather the eucharistic 'action' at the lectern and
the altar. The use of candles to highlight the Liturgies of Word
and Sacrament will vary between different settings but as long
as the basic principle is clear, there is considerable room for
experimentation.

Questions for Reflection and Discussion

• What types of bread and wine do you use in your church?
  How satisfactory are these for their purpose in the
  Eucharist?
• What types of vessels are used? How satisfactory are
  these?
• Is there any excess clutter that needs to be removed?

13

Vestments

Necessity

There is some reflection and discussion in the Church of England at the moment about the use of what are often called 'robes' for presiding at worship. In some churches, they are viewed as a tiresome anachronism and have been dispensed with.

For a variety of reasons, practical and theological, it is important that presidents and deacons at the Eucharist should wear vestments. Vestments add colour and dignity to the celebration, highlighting the liturgical season. They help stop the individual style of the president's body, dress and, perhaps, personality detracting from the worship that is being offered.

The tradition in some parishes dictates that vestments be fairly minimal. If this is so, an alb and stole are perfectly adequate. Surplices and copes are not appropriate for the celebration of the Eucharist.

Whatever vestments are worn, it is important that they should be kept on *throughout the service* and not changed at different stages. The complicated procedure experienced in some churches of removing and putting back on stoles, copes and chasubles at various points in the Eucharist can be nothing other than a distraction from the prayer that is being offered.

Style

'Dear Fathers ... Now we have moved from the era of gin, backbiting and lace to the era of gin, backbiting and box pleats ...' So legend has it one speaker at a conference on 'renewal' began a speech. There has, of course, been a revolution in the ecclesiastical sartorial world, but the comment implies that what we wear in church is little more than a churchmanship badge, and that vestments are not really to be taken seriously.

The fundamental principle about vestments in the liturgy is this: the liturgical space should be as simple as possible so that the colour is brought into the arena by the ministers wearing vestments of grace and elegance that enrich the eucharistic action. Modern thinking emphasizes the beauty and drape of the material, not complex embroidery that can be applied to a stiff board! Indeed it is to be hoped that the days when the clergy seemed to be trussed up like chickens have utterly gone!

The alb

The alb is the 'white garment' in Revelation, which reminds us of the baptismal garment. Investment in a good matching set of albs, made of high quality material for servers and clergy, is a use of resources well worth making, and it may well be that the person who is going to wear an alb will be prepared to buy it and look after it.

A fuller style is more elegant for clergy and servers of both sexes. Albs need to be long enough: just 5 cm off the ground; albs at half-mast look as comic as trousers! It is a mistake to be tempted by girdles, especially for the portly: the beauty should be in the hang of the material. Badges, ribbons and so on should not be worn on top of the alb. Simplicity and the symbolism of the white garment are the key considerations. It may be useful to find a style that needs an amice as this brings uniformity and tidiness round the neck and the amice can be cleaned separately with greater frequency than the alb.

The stole

Teaching Point

The stole

The stole has a functional origin: it came into being as a scarf to keep neck and upper body warm and as a face covering when one died. St Ambrose in AD 386 wrote that St Lazarus was wrapped in an *orarium*, or scarf, as he was laid in the crypt. By the fourth century it had been adopted by Roman society as a sign of dignity similar to that of public honours, but early Christian writers attach to it the symbolism of Christ washing the feet of the twelve and thus the stole is a distinctive sign of commissioning at ordination: in the deacon's case to proclaim the word of God; and in the priest's to preside at the eucharistic assembly, to absolve and to bless.

The deacon wears the stole like a sash, over the left shoulder, fastened at the hip on the right side. It is worn like this as a reminder of the Roman servant who, because his master had no pockets in his toga, accompanied him with a handkerchief over his right arm. This, of course, is the origin of the maniple, the wearing of which is now rare and not recommended in this book.

The priest wears the stole round the neck, with its two ends hanging down (not, in modern times, crossed over).

The stole is worn over the alb. Once again, simplicity is important and stoles should match. The modern stole is long, usually reaching to the shinbone. It should never be more than 11.5 cm wide, and the cloth must be the best affordable.

The chasuble

Teaching Point

The chasuble

The chasuble is a symbol of the compassion of Christ. Whereas the other vestments, on the whole, were adapted from the garments of the people in charge, the chasuble is derived from the poncho-like cloak of the worker who needed protection from the elements. Its design allowed the farmer to work in the fields even when it was raining because he could see down in front of his cloak to watch what he was doing. St Paul left one of these in Troas (2 Tim. 4.13). For hundreds of years this garment had been worn on the backs of peasants and workers, and it was not until the middle of the fourth century that it was adopted by Roman society largely due to the influence of the Church. The original form was conical, free flowing and long, extending over the hands and to the ankle, but in the course of time was modified into the Gothic style that is common today.

Like the stole, the chasuble should be of the best possible quality. Its colour should be strong enough to emphasize the season or liturgical occasion without too many fussy patterns (see below). Some chasubles today have a strong 1970s look to them (waving sheaves of corn, smiling fish, etc.) and their use may need to be reviewed: sometimes, ironically, older vestments look far less dated. The cut and style of the chasuble needs to be ample and flowing but not exaggeratedly large. Where possible, it is good if stoles of matching material can be provided.

Teaching Point

Other vestments

In some parishes, in addition to the stole, the deacon may wear a dalmatic. This and the chasuble must be of the same material and style so as to indicate the collaborative liturgical ministry of the president and the deacon. The dalmatic takes its name from Dalmatia, a historic region of Croatia, along the Adriatic Sea. In the early centuries it was the garb of persons of rank and prestige in civil society but in AD 332 Pope St Sylvester made it the garment of the order of deacons.

The tunicle was the vestment of the sub-deacon when these existed in the Church. It can be distinguished from the dalmatic, the vestment of the deacon, as it has one horizontal bar across the front and back rather than two. If sacristy cupboards contain such a garment perhaps the crucifer might wear it, so long as it matches the vestments of the clergy.

Colour

It is outside the scope of this book to give detailed guidance on the important subject of celebrating the seasons in the liturgical year (see introduction). However, bearing in mind the comments already made in this chapter about the role of colour in the celebration of the Eucharist, the following thumbnail sketch may be helpful:

Colour	Season	Day	Symbolism
Green	Ordinary Time		Hope, everlasting life, fidelity
White	Christmas, Easter, BVM Feasts, Virgins	Conversion of Paul, Birth of JB	Joy, exuberance, celebration, resurrection, victory, purity, innocence
Gold	Solemn Feasts		Same as white
Red	Pentecost, Good Friday	Palm Sunday, Martyrs	Holy Spirit, suffering of Our Lord of the Apostles, blood of martyrs
Violet (Purple)	Advent, Lent	Funerals, All Souls' Day	Sorrow, mourning, repentance, penance
Black	All Souls' Day (perhaps)		Mourning and death
Rose	Gaudete (3rd in Advent) and Laetare (4th in Lent) Sundays		Subdued joy

Questions for Reflection and Discussion

- How much can you tell about people from the clothes they wear?
- Take all the vestments out of the vestment chest or cupboard in your church. What condition are they in? What

are they trying to symbolize? How attractive/unattractive are they? Do they need to be repaired, cleaned or replaced?

Additional Note: Incense

Incense is a symbol of the prayers of the community, focused in a particular way. This book argues throughout for an uncluttered approach to worship, emphasizing space, silence and simplicity. However, sometimes this is the last thing that the use of incense seems to encourage. Individual censings – three singles for a priest or bishop, two for a deacon, one for lay people and so on – derive from a Tridentine and hierarchical view of the church. They nowadays tend to seem quite comic and utterly inappropriate, as are the exaggerated and grotesque methods of swinging the censer that some servers and clergy often appear to enjoy.

Incense is used at three key places in the Eucharist:

First of all, in the *entrance procession*. The most ancient use of incense – which was taken over from the basilican tradition where the lawyers were preceded by incense wherever they went, rather as the Royal Family and our High Court judges wear nosegays – was in procession. In Christian worship today, using incense in the procession emphasizes the fact that people are coming together, gathering for prayer and worship.

Next, incense is used to *bring honour to the words of the gospel*, the good news of Jesus Christ. The reader of the gospel censes the gospel book just before reading from it.

Third, and finally, because the Eucharist is a service of word and sacrament, the *bread and wine that are soon to be consecrated* are censed as well.

In addition, the following are often also censed: the *altar* upon which the bread and wine will be consecrated and the *cross*, since it is the cross that stands at the heart of the Eucharist and the *congregation* – the worshipping community is also made holy in the Eucharist.

More detailed instruction about use of incense at these points is available in part 5 on movement.

Another possibility is for incense not to be carried around but placed in a bowl with lighted charcoal somewhere in the sanctuary. At appropriate moments, such as the gospel and the offertory, incense can be put on the burning coals.

Some final practical points: incense originally smells sweet but it can lose its odour and, if it does so, it will no longer produce a pleasant smell. It therefore needs to be kept in an airtight container at all times except when being used in a service. Incense is burned on charcoal and if the charcoal is allowed to burn without any incense on it (or with incense that has been burnt out) it will smell acrid and unpleasant. This should therefore be avoided (possibly by taking the thurible or pot in which the incense is being burned right away from the worship space when it is not needed). In addition, placing the charcoals on silver foil inside a pot or thurible will provide a cleaner burn and, consequently, a sweeter smell. Like incense, charcoal should be kept in an airtight container otherwise it can go damp and crumbly.

Teaching Point

Incense and sacrifice

The burning of incense is a time-honoured feature of Christian worship: one that can be traced back to the early days of the Church and, beyond that, to the Old Testament in which incense is repeatedly mentioned. The use of incense in sacrifices in the temple in Jerusalem has caused some Christians to reject it as a part of Christian worship. If the one perfect sacrifice of Christ on the cross puts an end to the sacrificial system (cf. the Letter to the Hebrews) then, it is argued, sacrificial images and practices are not appropriate in relation to the Eucharist. Against this, catholic sacramental theology would argue that, although the sacrifice of Christ is indeed unique and unrepeatable, it is made present and shown forth (not simply remembered) whenever the Eucharist is celebrated. In the Eucharist, the offering of the Church, the body of Christ, is joined to the sacrifice of Christ, the head of the Church (cf. Col. 1.18).

More utilitarian justifications for the use of incense are sometimes offered. It represents prayers rising to God and, by providing something to smell, enables the Eucharist to engage all five senses in worship, not just four of them.

Part 5

Movement

14

Liturgical Commentary

This chapter aims to give a basic commentary on the action of
the Eucharist, following *Common Worship*, Order One,
which can be read in conjunction with the step-by-step guide
in the next chapter.

The Gathering

Greeting

The words 'The Lord be with you/And also with you' or
'Grace, mercy and peace ...' are the liturgical greeting for the
Eucharist, in which the congregation are being welcomed in
God's name. It is generally a good idea for the president, after
the greeting, to introduce the Eucharist, but the liturgical
greeting is the context for any further welcome or introduction and should always come first. An introduction to the
Eucharist might say something about the theme of the service
(such as, for example, its being a Dedication Festival, All
Saints, or Harvest) or reflect briefly on the readings or some
aspect of what people are doing when they celebrate the
Eucharist. Whatever the case, it probably needs to be succinct:
no more than three or four sentences which, if possible, lead
naturally into the Prayers of Penitence.

The Collect for Purity

Before the Prayers of Penitence, *Common Worship* has a prayer of preparation (traditionally known as the Collect for Purity) which may be said. It may be felt that this prayer is better used by clergy and congregation alike as a prayer of preparation *before* the Eucharist begins because, excellent as it certainly is, it slightly interrupts the flow of the service.

Prayers of Penitence

The president is not recommended to use lengthy introductions to the Prayers of Penitence, still less recite the whole of the Ten Commandments. It will almost always be more effective for the Prayers of Penitence to be introduced simply and in the president's own words after introducing the Eucharist.

A decision will need to be taken about which of the available forms of the Prayers of Penitence to use. As a general rule, it is probably better to use one of the first two (longer) forms in *Common Worship* at a sung celebration.

The third (shorter) form is often called the Penitential Kyries. These use short sentences before each part of the Kyrie Eleison. An example of this is:

Lord Jesus, you raise us to new life, Lord have mercy.
Lord, have mercy.

Lord Jesus, you forgive our sins, Christ have mercy.
Christ, have mercy.

Lord Jesus, you feed us with your body and blood.
Lord have mercy. Lord, have mercy.

Since the Penitential Kyrie is shorter, it is more suitable for said celebrations.

The Kyrie Eleison can be said or sung before the absolution, making the Kyries, as they traditionally are, part of the penitential rite of the Eucharist. Alternatively, the Kyries can come after the absolution. If Penitential Kyries have been used, it is unnecessary to say or sing the Kyrie Eleison again.

Whichever form it is, it never sounds good for the president to make announcements like, 'We will now say form B of the confession.' If more than one is printed, simply saying the opening words will be enough.

The Absolution

Throughout this absolution, the words *you* and *your* are italicized in *Common Worship*. This is because the president will need to decide whether to say *us* and *our* instead. It is perhaps the case that *us* and *our* forms are preferable because, unlike in a sacramental confession, at this point in the Eucharist, the whole congregation (including the president) is confessing sins *together*.

The Roman Rite provides an alternative form of absolution, shorter and particularly suitable for said celebrations:

> May almighty God have mercy on us, forgive us our sins and bring us to everlasting life. Amen.

The Collect

Traditionally, the words *Let us pray* used to come right at the start of the Eucharist (confession, Kyrie, Gloria, etc. being later additions). These words are therefore very important: they form a point at which the prayer of the congregation can be focused (literally *collected*) before the Liturgy of the Word. In order to enable this to happen, they should never be left out. The task of the collect is to articulate the prayers of the people and time is needed for this to happen. Therefore, there should be a short silent period between 'Let us pray' and the start of the collect.

The Liturgy of the Word

The end of the readings

In the Latin Mass, after each reading the reader says 'Verbum Domini'. This literally means 'the word of the Lord' but is normally translated, 'This is the word of the Lord.' Alternative endings might be 'Hear the word of the Lord' or 'For the word of the Lord', both followed by 'Thanks be to God.' Another alternative is simply to say nothing and let the word of the Lord speak for itself.

Gestures at the gospel

The reason for the sign of the cross being made on the book, forehead, breast and lips is that 'the words of the Gospel renew the sign of the Cross made at baptism. It touches the lips, like the glowing coal of Isaiah's seraphim (Is. 6.6–7). It cleanses and converts the heart' (Andrew Burnham, *The Deacon at the Eucharist*, p. 13).

After the sermon

The importance of silence in the liturgy is emphasized throughout this book. After the sermon, it will almost always be a good idea for the preacher and everyone else to sit down and then leave a pause for the congregation to digest what has been said.

The creed

- *Importance* Many congregations find the Nicene Creed a rather cumbersome thing to have to say at this point in the service, which is presumably why the *Common Worship* rubric allows some (shorter) alternatives. However, Anglican liturgies have traditionally given a great deal of importance to the creed in worship (since in the *BCP* the congregation not only says the creed at the Eucharist but also at Morning and Evening Prayer) and it is very important that this statement of the Christian faith keeps a central place in the liturgy. However, there may be some circumstances in which a shorter affirmation of faith (said or sung) is appropriate and the creed is normally omitted on days that are not Sundays or major feasts.

- *Facing east* In some churches, there is a custom of facing east during the creed. This has some echoes of ancient baptismal practice but it is difficult, strictly speaking, to see the reason for its enduring popularity in the Anglican offices and Eucharist. At the Eucharist, of course, the congregation are likely to be facing east in any case. In particular, the president should not turn to face east at this point. In general, good Eucharistic presidency is best achieved by the president remaining at the chair and keeping reasonably still, avoiding unnecessary movement except when at the lectern or the altar.

The Liturgy of the Sacrament

The peace

- *Introduction* There are a number of forms of introduction to the peace and it is good to vary these according to season, etc. It is also possible for the president to *ad-lib* these words, though, except for the very confident, the words will need to be prepared in advance. The exact form in which the peace will be introduced does not need to be printed in the service book.
- *History* Many people assume that the peace is a 'touchy-feely' addition to the Eucharist, which was invented in the 1970s, but nothing could be further from the truth. In fact, in the oldest post-biblical account of the Eucharist we have, that of Justin Martyr (see Teaching Point on page 51), we are told that 'At the end of the prayers, we salute one another with a kiss.'

- *Position* There are a number of possible positions suggested by *Common Worship*. Of these, the best seem to be the Ambrosian/Anglican position (after the intercessions) or the 'Roman' position (after the Lord's Prayer). It is not clear that the peace appropriately forms part of the gathering or the dismissal.
- *The Peace of Christ* In some churches the rather anarchic nature of the peace, while questionable according to strict liturgical rules, can be quite a moving experience and a 'sign of contradiction' in a fragmented and individualistic society.

    However, it is important to remember that when the peace is shared at the Eucharist, it is a sharing of Christ's peace and not the moment for displays of individual affection in which some are greeted with hugs and kisses and others with rather cold handshakes.

Offertory procession

Many churches have an offertory procession, in which members of the congregation bring up bread and wine and these are received by the president, deacon or a server. These have been criticized on the grounds that they obscure the important truth that we come to God empty-handed. However, they do carry very positive messages about the ways in which our lives and labour are offered to God in the Eucharist. An offertory procession also encourages a sense of participation in the liturgy.

In many churches the collection will also be taken at this point in the service. Although, in terms of the *Book of Common Prayer*, there is some justification for 'alms and oblations' being offered together, the unfortunate result is that this often leads to a small procession of two or three people carrying bread, wine and water and a much larger procession of people with collection bags. This defeats the point of the offertory procession and loses the symbolism of the bread and wine being brought to the altar. Different congregations will manage this in different ways but if these gifts are going to be presented, it will be important to think about what messages may be given.

Setting up the altar

- *How to do it* The way that this is described in the next chapter may look complicated when described on paper but it is in fact extremely simple. If these instructions are followed, the process of setting up the altar will look dignified and unfussy and will be relatively quick.
- *The look of the altar* when it has been set up is even more important. In many churches it becomes very cluttered with, for example, burse and veil, a variety of different books and pieces of paper, the vicar's reading glasses and so on. This destroys what the congregation needs to see: bread and wine. In addition to the altar candles (and even they can stand on the floor if they are tall enough) all that needs to be on the altar during the Eucharistic Prayer is bread, wine and one book. Whatever vessels are in use, one main paten and one main chalice should stand out as the focus of attention.
- *At times when the Eucharist is not being celebrated* the altar is best kept completely clear. It is not, for example, a suitable stand for an open Bible (a lectern, on the other hand, might be).

Prayers at the preparation of the table

A general guideline is that at a *said* celebration these prayers should be used to accentuate the 'taking' action (see Teaching Point on page 113). However, when the Eucharist is *sung* and offertory processions, servers, etc. make the taking action more obvious, it is preferable for the president to say them quietly while the hymn is being sung so that, at the end of the hymn, it is possible to start immediately with the dialogue at the beginning of the Eucharistic Prayer.

Eucharistic preface

A large variety of these are provided in the new liturgical materials. There is early Church precedent for the preface, or at least some of it, being ad-libbed by the president and this might give an opportunity to articulate particular thanks-givings in the preface and incorporate these in the Eucharistic Prayer. As is noted in an earlier chapter, prayers of thanks-giving belong much more naturally here than in the inter-cessions.

Saying the Eucharistic Prayer

In line with the overall approach of this book, we suggest that the way the president prays the Eucharistic Prayer should be marked by simplicity and dignity. To achieve this, the president will need to pay attention to:

- *Gesture* In contrast to the over-fussy movements that one often experiences (for example, complex lifting up of objects and making signs of the cross at different times and in different ways), this great prayer should be offered with only a few strong and simple gestures at key points, which are indicated in the next chapter.
- *Voice* is also important. This should certainly not be deadpan but not artificially impregnated with meaning and sincerity either. Let these wonderful words speak for themselves and pray them simply, reverently and naturally. It is helpful for presidents to watch a recording of them-selves from time to time, to ensure that the parsonical voice has not crept in.
- *Book* It is good to be able to arrange the altar book so that the Eucharistic Prayer can be said/sung *without* distracting page turning by the president or a server at key moments (such as in the middle of the Words of Institution).

Eucharistic acclamations

- *Variety* Those who are compiling service books for different seasons in the year may want to use different acclamations according to the season; for example, 'Dying you destroyed our death; rising you restored our life, Lord Jesus come in glory' might be used during Advent and 'Lord, by your cross and resurrection you have set us free; you are the saviour of the world' in Eastertide.
- *Announcement* As emphasized elsewhere, it is not good liturgical practice to say, for example, 'We will now use the first acclamation.' This will disrupt the flow of the Eucharistic Prayer. *Common Worship* has provided different introductions to each acclamation so that this can be avoided. In some churches the president says these words. In others, it is seen as the task of the deacon as it is about the enabling/facilitating of the congregation, which is central to the deacon's role.

The Lord's Prayer

- *Introduction* The Lord's Prayer is an important transition point in the Eucharist because, whereas the Eucharistic Prayer is mainly said by the president alone with the congregation participating silently, in the Lord's Prayer and what comes after it, the congregation participates in a more vocal way. *Common Worship* has been rather sparing with introductions to the Lord's Prayer, having only:

  As our Saviour taught us, so we pray ...

  It is a good idea to vary the introductions so as to add variety and, more importantly, to bring out different aspects of this great prayer. Some alternative introductions are:

  Jesus taught us to call God our Father, so in faith and trust we say ...

  or

> *Let us pray for the coming of the Kingdom in the words our Saviour gave us ...*

or

> *He is present among us who taught us ...*

or (with children)

> *Let's say together the prayer that Jesus taught us ...*

Alternatively, the president might introduce the prayer in some other words.

- *Version Common Worship* gives an alternative (modern) version of the Lord's Prayer. Although the modern form has some advantages (such as consistency with the language of the rest of the service) it is poorly translated into modern English (for example, *hallowed be your name – hallowed* is not a modern English word). More importantly, this is the one prayer in the Eucharist which non-churchgoers still have a reasonable chance of knowing. In any case, it is best to choose one version and stick to it and, as at other places, for the president *not* to say things like, 'We will now say the Lord's Prayer in the traditional version.'

The Prayer of Humble Access

After the invitation to communion, *Common Worship* suggests that either the traditional or updated Prayer of Humble Access be said before people receive communion. It may be felt that, like the Collect for Purity at the beginning of the service, this prayer works best as a prayer of *preparation* before the Eucharist begins and that the Prayer of Humble Access is repetitious if the words 'Lord, I am not worthy to receive you ...' are said before receiving communion. However, the attitudes of reverence and awe before the gift of the sacrament that this prayer embodies are important and perhaps especially suited to the seasons of Advent and Lent.

Communion arrangements

The simplest way for communion to be received is either by the congregation standing around or in front of the altar or by people coming forward to receive from a central station in front of the altar. Some congregations are very keen on receiving while kneeling down and this wish must be treated sensitively (it certainly has good warrant in the *Book of Common Prayer*). Whatever the case, communion should be received at the *same* altar at which the Eucharist has been celebrated (except on big occasions, when different 'stations' are needed).

Communion silence

Throughout this book, the importance of silence in the liturgy is emphasized. Nowhere is it more important than at this moment, after communion has been received, that there should be a period of absolute silence, with no movement by clergy, servers, etc. Obviously, in some churches this will be difficult to achieve and it may be that the president needs to ask specifically for it to happen.

The Dismissal

Blessing

- *Words* Before the dismissal, *Common Worship* provides a blessing and says that a seasonal blessing may be used. A number of these are provided in seasonal materials accompanying the Anglican liturgies and it is obviously a good idea to make use of the seasonal variations. The Roman Rite has a short and simple blessing that is particularly useful for said Eucharists: *May almighty God bless you, the Father, the Son and the Holy Spirit.* This is also a good one to have in the repertoire.

- *Actions* Recommended hand movement for the blessing is given in the next chapter. Like all the gestures recommended in this book, this is a simple and powerful one and it is important that the president makes the sign of the cross at this point. Some important things to avoid are:

1 using the forefinger and middle finger only;
2 making the sign of the cross three times (both 1 and 2 are traditionally done only by bishops);
3 making complex or exaggerated movements involving both hands;
4 holding a single hand outstretched – this looks like a Nazi salute;
5 having one hand touching the altar while making the sign of the cross – this is pointless.

The congregation are blessed by the cross of Christ and this is made clear by the president making a simple, clear and large sign of the cross over the rest of the congregation.

Dismissal

The words 'Thanks be to God' are a translation of the Latin *Deo Gratias*, which are the traditional words at the end of the Eucharist. It is recommended that, whichever words are used for the dismissal, the response should *always* be 'Thanks be to God.'

Teaching Point

Taking, blessing, breaking, distributing

Liturgical scholars, notably the Anglican Benedictine monk Dom Gregory Dix (1901–52), emphasize the importance of the 'fourfold action' of the Eucharist. The bread and wine are (1) taken (2) blessed (3) broken and (4) distributed. Such actions can be traced back to the New Testament accounts of the Last Supper itself and also to events that appear to prefigure it, such as the feeding of the five thousand (cf. Mark 6.30–44). Although liturgical scholarship has, in some ways, moved on since Dix's time, this insight remains extremely valuable. In any celebration of the Eucharist, the integrity of these four actions needs to be preserved and highlighted.

15

Step by Step Guide

This section gives the outline for a sung celebration of the Eucharist according to the Church of England's *Common Worship* Order One. It uses a set of 'default' options, in other words those that seem obvious. Clearly, when other options are used or when it is a said Eucharist, things will need to be varied appropriately.

Two slightly different positions for the president's hands are referred to at various stages. These have been called:

1 *The greeting position*: hands apart and outstretched towards the congregation.
2 *The praying* (orans) *position*: hands apart and outstretched pointing upwards.

At other times the president's hands should be kept together.

The Gathering

A few moments of silence and perhaps a prayer are strongly recommended before the Eucharist begins.

If incense is being used, the thurible is brought to the president before the service begins. The president puts incense on the hot charcoals and then blesses it, making the sign of the cross.

An entrance hymn is sung as the ministers come to the altar.

The president and deacon approach the altar; the president with hands together and the deacon holding the gospel book. When they reach the altar, the ministers stop (with the president in the middle and the deacon a little to the president's right). They both bow (or genuflect if the sacrament is reserved behind the altar). The deacon places the gospel book on the altar (if there is no deacon, the gospel book might be on the altar from the outset) and leads the president round to the 'working side' of the altar. The deacon places the gospel book centrally on the altar. The president and deacon both kiss the altar (again, with the president in the middle and the deacon a little to the president's right). The president kisses the altar with hands apart on the altar but the deacon keeps hands together while kissing the altar.

If the altar is to be censed at this point (and it is not strictly necessary if it will be censed again, along with the gifts at the offertory) the president takes the thurible and censes the altar, with the deacon walking slightly in front. To cense the altar, the president holds the chains just below the disc in the left hand and the chains just above the bowl in the right hand (hands reversed if left-handed). The president walks around the altar, with left hand held at chest level and right hand gently swinging the bowl of the thurible (there is no need to 'chink' the chains). The president and deacon may stop to cense the cross at a convenient place. This is done by giving the thurible three double swings all in the same direction towards the cross.

After this, the president and deacon go to their seats until the end of the hymn.

The Greeting

The president makes the sign of the cross while saying:

President   In the name of the Father, and of the Son, and
              of the Holy Spirit.

All   **Amen.**

The president, with arms in the greeting position says:

President   Grace, mercy and peace
              from God our Father
              and the Lord Jesus Christ
              be with you.
All   **And also with you.**

*The president introduces the Eucharist and then the Prayers of
Penitence.*

Prayers of Penitence

The president introduces the Prayers of Penitence.

President   Almighty God,

All   **Our heavenly Father, we have sinned against
              you through our own fault, in thought and
              word and deed and in what we have left
              undone. We are heartily sorry and repent of
              all our sins. For your son, our Lord Jesus
              Christ's sake, forgive us all that is past and
              grant that we may serve you in newness of life
              to the glory of your name. Amen.**

President   Lord have Mercy.

All   **Lord have mercy.**

President	Christ have Mercy.
All	**Christ have mercy.**
President	Lord have Mercy.
All	**Lord have mercy.**

President   Almighty God, who forgives all who truly repent, have mercy upon *you*, pardon and deliver *you* from all *your* sins, confirm and strengthen *you* in all goodness, and keep *you* in life eternal; through Jesus Christ our Lord.

All   **Amen.**

During the absolution, if it is in the 'you' form, the president may make the sign of the cross over the congregation. This is done in a similar way to the blessing at the end of the Eucharist, which is described below.

Gloria in Excelsis

On Sundays and feast days and other days when it seems particularly appropriate, Gloria in Excelsis is then said or sung.

All   **Glory to God in the highest, and peace to his people on earth.**

Lord God, heavenly King, almighty God and Father, we worship you, we give you thanks, we praise you for your glory.

Lord Jesus Christ, only Son of the Father, Lord God, Lamb of God, you take away the sin of the world: have mercy on us; you are seated at the right hand of the Father: receive our prayer. For you alone are the Holy One, you alone are the Lord, you alone are the

Most High, Jesus Christ, with the Holy Spirit,
in the glory of God the Father. Amen.

*During the Prayers of Penitence and the Gloria, the president
and deacon remain standing at the chair with hands together.*

The Collect

*The president introduces the collect with hands together, say-
ing 'Let us pray', followed perhaps by a more specific bidding
(such as 'Let us pray for the knowledge of God's love in our
lives ...') and then a short period of silence. The president then
says or sings the collect with hands in the praying position
until '... through Jesus Christ our Lord ...', at which point the
hands are joined.*

The Liturgy of the Word

Readings

After each of the readings before the gospel:

Reader   This is the Word of the Lord.

All   **Thanks be to God.**

The psalm follows the Old Testament reading.

*A sung acclamation heralds the gospel reading. This could be
a (short) hymn or, best of all, an alleluia.*

*If incense is being used, the president puts it on the charcoal
during the acclamation and blesses it silently, making the sign
of the cross.*

If the deacon is to be given a blessing before reading the gospel, the deacon goes to the president without the gospel book, bows in front of the president and says, 'Give me your blessing.' The president blesses the deacon, making the sign of the cross (as for the final blessing – see below) and saying quietly, 'May the Lord be in your heart and on your lips that you may worthily proclaim his holy gospel in the Name of the Father and of the Son and of the Holy Spirit.' The deacon takes the gospel book from the altar and goes to the place where the gospel will be read. While walking, the deacon holds the book up at about eye level so that it is visible to the congregation.

If there is no deacon, the president or assistant priest follows the same procedure but instead of going for a blessing bows for a short prayer in front of the altar: 'Lord, be in my heart and on my lips that I may worthily proclaim your holy gospel.'

There may be a procession to the place where the gospel is being read. If so, this should not involve the cross since it is the book of the Gospels that, at this stage in the service, represents Christ.

Gospel reading

The gospel reader, with hands together, says:

Reader   The Lord be with you.

All   **And also with you.**

Reader   Hear the Gospel of our Lord Jesus Christ
           according to N.

All   **Glory to you, O Lord.**

*While saying the above words, the gospel reader makes the
sign of the cross first on the book at the start of the gospel,
then on the lips and then on the breast.*

*If incense is being used, the book is then censed with three
double swings, two to the centre, then two to the left and then
two to the right.*

When the gospel is finished:

Reader   This is the Gospel of the Lord.

All   **Praise to you, O Christ.**

*After saying this, the gospel reader kisses the book in the same
place where the sign of the cross was made on it before the
reading.*

*After the gospel reading, the deacon and servers return to their
places. The deacon places the gospel book not on the floor but
possibly on one of the following three places:*

• *on the credence table;*

• *on the altar for the rest of the service but open and facing
  outwards, not closed as before, since the gospel has now
  been opened by the reading of it in the liturgy;*

• *on the lectern but open, as above.*

Sermon

A period of silence follows the sermon.

*The president introduces the creed, perhaps with some 'bridg-
ing' words connecting the readings and sermon with the creed
or, for example, 'Let us affirm our faith in God, Father, Son
and Holy Spirit' or 'Let us proclaim the faith we share.'*

The creed

The Prayers of Intercession

The Liturgy of the Eucharist

A somewhat different combination of patens and chalices than recommended in chapter 12 is presupposed here, so as to reflect what is more common practice. These guidelines presuppose a paten for the 'priest's host' and a ciborium and two chalices will be in use rather than, as is preferable, one large paten, one chalice and a flagon. It is hoped that the guidelines will be reasonably easily adaptable.

The peace

The president, remaining at the chair, introduces the peace with a suitable sentence and then says:

President   The peace of the Lord be always with you.

All   **And also with you.**

The deacon (or, if there is no deacon, the president) then says:

Deacon   Let us offer one another a sign of peace.

An offertory hymn or song is sung during the preparation of the altar.

If a deacon is preparing the altar:

1 *The deacon lays out the corporal on the altar, folding it outwards so as to catch any crumbs.*

2 *The deacon receives the ciborium from a server and places it on the top left square of the corporal.*

3 *The deacon receives the main chalice. The deacon takes the paten with the large wafer off the chalice, laying the paten by the side of the corporal and putting both of the chalices near the edge of the altar.*

4 *The deacon takes the wine flagon and pours wine into both chalices while they are standing on the altar. (This will help to prevent spillages and looks better than filling up the chalices in mid-air.)*

5 *With the chalices still standing on the altar, the deacon adds a small amount of water to each chalice. While adding the water, the deacon says quietly: 'By the mystery of this water and wine, may we come to share in the divinity of Christ who humbled himself to share in our humanity.' The deacon puts the second chalice on the top right square of the corporal and then the main chalice by the side of the paten.*

6 *The president comes to the altar. The deacon hands the president the paten. Taking the paten and raising it slightly above the corporal, the president says quietly the first of the* Blessed are you *prayers, to which the deacon responds, 'Blessed be God for ever.' The president then places the paten on the corporal. The deacon hands the president the main chalice. Taking the chalice and raising it slightly above the corporal, the president says quietly the second* Blessed are you *prayer, to which the deacon responds, 'Blessed be God for ever.' The president then places the chalice on the corporal.*

If there is no deacon and the president is preparing the altar:

1 *The president lays out the corporal on the altar, folding it outwards.*

2 *The president takes the ciborium from a server and places it on the top left square of the corporal. The president takes the paten and the large wafer off the chalice, leaving the chalices to one side. The president takes the paten and, raising it slightly above the corporal, says quietly the first of the* Blessed are you *prayers and then places the paten on the corporal.*

3 *The president puts both chalices at the edge of the altar, takes the flagon of wine from a server and pours it into both chalices while they are standing on the altar.*

4 *With the chalices still standing on the altar, the president takes the water flagon and adds a small amount of water to each chalice. (There is no need to bless the water.) While adding the water, the president says quietly, 'By the mystery of this water and wine, may we come to share in the divinity of Christ who humbled himself to share in our humanity.' The president takes the second chalice and places it in the top right square of the corporal. The president then takes the main chalice and, raising it slightly above the corporal, says quietly the second* Blessed are you *prayer and then places the chalice on the corporal.*

If incense is being used, after the gifts have been prepared, the thurible is brought to the president who puts incense on the charcoal and blesses it silently, making the sign of the cross. The president takes the thurible and censes the bread and wine with three double swings, two to the centre, then two to the left and then two to the right over the bread and wine. The president may then cense the altar and the cross. For guidance on how to do this, see page 115.

After the altar has been censed, the altar book (with the Eucharistic Prayer) is placed to the left of the corporal.

If incense is being used, the deacon or a server may go to the front of the sanctuary and bow slightly to everyone in it, who all bow back. The deacon censes everyone in the sanctuary (together) and then the rest of the congregation, with three double swings, two to the centre, then two to the left and then two to the right.

After the president and all in the sanctuary have been censed, a server brings the lavabo bowl and towel for the president's hands to be washed. While this is being done, the president says quietly, 'Lord, wash away my iniquity and cleanse me from my sin.'

The Eucharistic Prayer

The president stands behind the altar, with the deacon slightly to the right, standing or kneeling. The president, with arms in the greeting position says (or sings):

President   The Lord be with you.

All   **And also with you.**

The president keeps arms stretched out and perhaps lifts them slightly and says or sings:

President   Lift up your hearts.

All   **We lift them to the Lord.**

With arms still in the greeting position:

President   Let us give thanks to the Lord our God.

All   **It is right to give thanks and praise.**

The president says or sings the preface with arms in the praying position.

President Father, we give you thanks and praise
through your beloved Son, Jesus Christ, your
living Word,
through whom you have created all things;
who was sent by you in your great goodness
to be our Saviour.

  By the power of the Holy Spirit he took
flesh;
as your Son, born of the blessed Virgin, he
lived on earth and went about among us;
he opened wide his arms for us on the cross;
he put an end to death by dying for us;
and revealed the resurrection by rising to new
life;
so he fulfilled your will and won for you a
holy people.

  Therefore with angels and archangels,
and with all the company of heaven,
we proclaim your great and glorious name,
for ever praising you and *saying (or singing,
if the* Sanctus *and* Benedictus *are going to be
sung*):

All **Holy, holy, holy Lord,
God of power and might,
heaven and earth are full of your glory.
Hosanna in the highest.
Blessed is he who comes in the name of the
Lord.
Hosanna in the highest.**

*If the ciborium has a lid on it and the chalices have palls on
them (generally, these are unnecessary), these can all be
removed during the Benedictus and left off for the rest of the
Eucharistic Prayer.*

President   Lord, you are holy indeed, the source of all
                 holiness;
                 grant that by the power of your Holy Spirit

the president stretches out both hands over the bread and wine

                 these gifts of bread and wine
                 may be to us the body and blood

*the president makes a single cross over the bread and wine
while saying the words 'body and blood'*

                 of our Lord Jesus Christ;
                 who, in the same night that he was betrayed,
                 took bread

*the president picks up the large wafer and holds it slightly
above the paten during the next section:*

                 and gave you thanks; *(the president may
                 briefly look upwards)*
                 he broke it and gave it to his disciples, saying:
                 Take, eat; this is my body which is given for
                 you;
                 do this in remembrance of me.

*The president holds the consecrated bread (but not the paten)
up at eye level so that it can be seen by the congregation and
pauses briefly. After this, the host is placed on the paten again
and the president and deacon genuflect or bow.*

*(If incense is being used, the deacon or thurifer may do three
double swings as the consecrated bread is held up.)*

                 In the same way, after supper
                 he took the cup

the president picks up the main chalice (but not any of the other chalices) and continues to hold it slightly over the corporal during the next section:

and gave you thanks; *(the president may briefly look upwards)*
he gave it to them, saying:
    Drink this, all of you;
this is my blood of the new covenant,
which is shed for you and for many for the
forgiveness of sins.
Do this as often as you drink it,
in remembrance of me.

The president holds the chalice up at eye level so that it can be seen by the congregation and pauses very briefly. After the chalice is placed back on the corporal, the president and deacon genuflect or bow.

(If incense is being used, the deacon or thurifer may do three double swings as the chalice is held up.)

(As will have been noticed from these guidelines, there is no need during the Words of Institution for the president to touch the additional chalice(s) or pick up the ciborium: the focus of attention should be the one bread and the one cup; the bread on the paten and the main chalice.)

The president or the deacon says or sings:

President   Great is the mystery of faith:

All   **Christ has died,**
               Christ is risen,
               Christ will come again.

For the remainder of the Eucharistic Prayer, until 'by whom and with whom ...' (the 'final doxology'), the president remains with arms in the praying position.

President   And so, Father, calling to mind his death on
                  the cross,
                  his perfect sacrifice made once for the sins of
                  the whole world;
                  rejoicing in his mighty resurrection and
                  glorious ascension,
                  and looking for his coming in glory,
                  we celebrate this memorial of our redemption.
                  As we offer you this our sacrifice of praise and
                  thanksgiving,
                  we bring before you this bread and this cup
                  and we thank you for counting us worthy
                  to stand in your presence and serve you.

                  Send the Holy Spirit on your people
                  and gather into one in your kingdom
                  all who share this one bread and one cup,
                  so that we, in the company of [N and] all the
                  saints,
                  may praise and glorify you for ever,
                  through Jesus Christ our Lord;

The following words (the doxology) *are the climax of the Eucharistic offering. With the left hand, the president picks up the paten and with the right, the main chalice and lifts them up to about chest level, looking upwards at the words, 'almighty Father'. If there is a deacon, the deacon lifts up the chalice and the president lifts up the paten.*

                  by whom and with whom and in whom,
                  in the unity of the Holy Spirit,
                  all honour and glory be yours, almighty
                  Father,
                  for ever and ever.
All   **Amen.**

The president replaces the consecrated bread and wine on the corporal.

The thurible is taken away at this point since it is not used for the remainder of the service.

The Lord's Prayer

The president says the first part of the prayer with hands in the praying position:

All   Our Father, who art in heaven
                  hallowed be thy name;
                  thy kingdom come
                  thy will be done
                  on earth as it is in heaven.
                  Give us this day our daily bread;
                  and forgive us our trespasses,
                  as we forgive those who trespass against us.
                  And lead us not into temptation;
                  but deliver us from evil.

For the last section of the prayer, the president's hands are joined:

                  For thine is the Kingdom,
                  the power and the glory
                  for ever and ever. Amen.

Breaking of the Bread

The president breaks the consecrated bread over the paten, visibly but without spreading crumbs.

President	We break this bread to share in the body of Christ.
All	**Though we are many, we are one body because we all share in one bread.**

During the Agnus Dei (Lamb of God), the president breaks any remaining bread that needs to be broken.

If extra chalices are needed to be filled from a flagon of consecrated wine, these are now brought to the altar.

If the reserved sacrament is to be collected from the aumbry or tabernacle, this is also done during the Agnus Dei.

Lay ministers who are going to distribute communion come near to the altar at this point.

All	**Lamb of God, you take away the sin of the world.** **Have mercy on us.** **Lamb of God, you take away the sin of the world.** **Have mercy on us.** **Lamb of God you take away the sin of the world.** **Grant us peace.**

Giving of Communion

President	Jesus is the Lamb of God who takes away the sins of the world. Blessed are those who are called to his supper.
All	**Lord, I am not worthy to receive you, but only say the word and I shall be healed.**

The president receives communion first in both kinds and then communicates the deacon, if present, or a chalice-bearer in both kinds. The president then communicates the rest of the congregation with the host and the deacon or chalice bearer with the chalice.

President
(or other   The body of Christ/The blood of Christ.
minister)

Communicant **Amen.**

During communion a hymn or hymns are sung.

After communion, any of the consecrated elements that are to be reserved in the aumbry or tabernacle need to be taken there straight away. This can be done by the deacon, a server or lay minister.

The eucharistic vessels are now washed up without delay. The ablutions are done by a deacon, if one is present or, if not, by the president, an assistant priest or a eucharistic minister. Since the ablutions are not part of the main action of the Eucharist, they should probably be done at a credence table or side altar.

1 *Any remaining bread and wine are consumed. Patens and ciboria are 'dry cleaned' with the finger and then put at the edge of the altar to be taken away.*

2 *The president/deacon holds out any vessels that need to be cleansed and a server pours a small amount of water into each one. It is unnecessary and time-consuming to use wine for the ablutions.*

3 *The president/deacon drinks the water in each vessel, turning it slightly while drinking for thorough cleaning and then wipes the inside with a purificator and, if the ablutions*

are being done at an altar, puts it at the edge of the altar so it can be taken away.

4 *After the final chalice is dried, the paten and pall (if there is one) are placed on top of the chalice and the corporal is placed on top of the pall and it is given to a server to take away.*

5 *A server takes the book away so that the altar is left completely clear.*

After the ablutions, the president and deacon return to the chair for the remainder of the service.

A period of silence is kept.

Prayer after Communion

The president stands at the chair and introduces the prayer after communion with hands together, saying 'Let us pray', but without a period of silence (there has already been silence after communion). The president then says the prayer with hands in the praying position until '... through Jesus Christ our Lord ...', at which point hands are joined.

A hymn or song may be sung either at this stage or after the dismissal.

After this:

President   Almighty God,

All   We thank you for feeding us
with the body and blood of your son, Jesus Christ.
Through him we offer you our souls and bodies
to be a living sacrifice.

**Send us out in the power of your spirit
to live and work to your praise and glory.**

During this prayer, the president's hands are joined.

Notices are given at this point.

The Dismissal

The president, with arms in the greeting position, says:

President   The Lord be with you.

All   **And also with you.**

President   The peace of God which passes all
             understanding keep your hearts and minds in
             the knowledge and love of God and of his son,
             Jesus Christ our Lord, and the blessing of
             almighty God, the Father, the Son and the
             Holy Spirit be among you and remain with
             you always.

All   **Amen.**

*During the blessing, the president makes the sign of the cross
over the people, once only, with the right hand and palm flat
(at right angles to the congregation) and the left hand resting
on the chest. The sign of the cross starts to be made with the
word 'Father' and continues during 'and of the Son and of the
Holy Spirit'.*

*After the blessing, the deacon or, if there is no deacon, the
president, with hands together says:*

President   Go in the peace of Christ.

All   **Thanks be to God.**

The president and deacon kiss the altar from the 'working side', the president in the middle with hands apart and the deacon to the president's right with hands together. After this, the clergy and other ministers bow (or genuflect) and then leave the altar.

Bibliography

On Anglican liturgy, the work of Michael Perham over the last twenty years or so provides a very valuable accompaniment to the whole range of *Common Worship* services. Perham's *New Handbook of Pastoral Liturgy* (SPCK, London, 2000) and its precursors cover some similar ground to this one, though from an angle that is less explicitly catholic than we attempt to be.

Do This by Bishop Kenneth Stevenson (Canterbury Press, Norwich, 2003) provides a commentary on the *Common Worship* Eucharist that ranges widely through historical, theological and practical issues and has an enormous range of reference. Timothy Gorringe's *The Sign of Love* (SPCK, London, 1997) places the Eucharist within its political context and would be an accessible and helpful guide for relatively educated congregations.

From a Roman Catholic perspective, Monsignor Peter Elliott's book, *Ceremonies of the Modern Roman Rite* (Ignatius Press, San Fransisco, 1995) is an invaluable and detailed guide to the sort of simple and dignified liturgy that we are recommending here. It is of particular use to those entrusted with the task of planning larger and therefore more complex services.

Jeffrey John's *Going for Growth* (Affirming Catholicism, London), is a short booklet in the Affirming Catholicism series. He identifies the Sunday Eucharist as the first priority in parish-based evangelism and gives sensible suggestions about its celebration. John integrates the Eucharist into a total mission strategy for small parishes based around the Sunday Eucharist, 'The Look of the Place' (that is, the church building), 'Ways In' (to the Christian Faith) and 'Induction and Teaching'.

On matters relating to church buildings and liturgical space, *Re-Pitching the Tent* by Richard Giles (Canterbury Press, Norwich, 2004) is invaluable. Cogently written and fully illustrated, it stimulates much thought on the relation between buildings and liturgy and makes important challenges to the vast majority of Anglican parishes. While the authors of this book have much sympathy for Giles's approach, a somewhat more gradualist one is advocated here. At the time of writing, a further volume from Richard Giles is due for publication. *Creating Common Worship* will be published by the Canterbury Press in 2004. Its focus is the celebration of the Eucharist in a re-ordered church building.

David Stancliffe's *God's Pattern* (SPCK, London, 2003) explores the relationship between the deep structures of the eucharistic liturgy and the shaping of ministry and life. The Liturgies of Word and Sacrament draw God's people into a pattern of engagement and transformation which have repercussions in many different areas.

On the ministry of a deacon, Andrew Burnham's *The Deacon at the Eucharist* (Church Union, London, 1992) is extremely useful, albeit now slightly dated in the era of *Common Worship*. Its accompanying volume *The Deacon's Ministry* edited by Christine Hall (Gracewing, Hertfordshire, 1992) gives further helpful reflection on the theology of the diaconate.

A fascinating article by Samuel Wells entitled *How Common Worship forms Local Character* explores the way in which different parts of the Eucharist are able to shape the members of the community who celebrate it. This can be found in *Studies in Christian Ethics* 15:1 (2002), published by T & T Clark, Edinburgh. All of the essays in this volume of the journal are devoted to the often-overlooked connections between liturgy and ethics. This approach is even more fully developed in *The Blackwell Companion to Christian Ethics*, edited by Stanley Haverwas and Samuel Wells (Blackwell Publishing, Oxford, 2004).

For reference, Paul Bradshaw (ed.) *The new SCM Dictionary of Liturgy and Worship* (SCM, London, 2002) is a most helpful guide.

The authors hope that this book will relate fairly easily to the eucharistic liturgies of all the provinces of the Anglican communion. However, since their background is specifically in the Church of England, the primary liturgical texts used have been Order One of *Common Worship, Services and Prayers for the Church of England* (Church House Publishing, London, 2000) and, to a lesser extent, the now superseded *Alternative Service Book* (Hodder & Stoughton, Sevenoaks, Kent, 1980).